"God works through Christian con. the question remains, *how?* How do we engage with the Holy Spirit in conversations that actually redeem the locust-eaten years of our lives? In this remarkable book, Rachael, Sonya and Diana invite us to listen in on their conversation as they 'lock arms to face the past' and 'search for and find the truth and beauty in one another.' *Listen In* is a pocket guide to authentic Christian community—a must-read for every person committed to being formed in the character of Christ."

Miriam (Mimi) Dixon, pastor, First Presbyterian Church of Golden, Colorado

"As a woman who is emotionally allergic to small talk, I deeply appreciate this book. It's a real-life example of what can happen when friends ask curious questions and cast a hopeful vision. I want to be the kind of friend that Rachael, Sonya and Diana are to one another and I'm thankful that they have generously let us listen in."

Emily P. Freeman, author of *A Million Little Ways* and *Grace for the Good Girl*

"Listening in to these richly nuanced conversations is more than just fascinating. It offers the hope that any woman can open her inner self with courage, pursue her friends with kind curiosity, and discover beauty hidden within her story. Rachael, Sonya and Diana beckon us all to similar conversations—with God delightedly listening in."

Nancy Groom, author of *Risking Intimacy*

"This is a one-of-a-kind book. You're invited to listen in as these women speak with rare courage and rich wisdom about how wounds from the past can, through the power of Jesus, be transformed into opportunities to relate well today."

Larry Crabb, psychologist and author of *Connecting* and *Shattered Dreams*

"In *Listen In*, my dear friend Rachael Crabb has given us a glimpse into the way that she builds deep friendships with women. The powerful and transformative conversations between the three women in this book provide a model and an inspiration for those of us who long for real spiritual connection. I highly recommend this book for individuals, prayer partners and small groups."

Elisa Morgan, author of *The Beauty of Broken* and cohost of *Discover the Word*

RACHAEL CRABB, SONYA REEDER & DIANA CALVIN

Foreword & Afterword by LARRY CRABB

Listen In

Building Faith and Friendship
Through Conversations That Matter

IVP Books

An imprint of InterVarsity Press
Downers Grove, Illinois

InterVarsity Press
P.O. Box 1400, Downers Grove, IL 60515-1426
ivpress.com
email@ivpress.com

InterVarsity Press® is the book-publishing division of InterVarsity Christian Fellowship/USA®, a movement of students and faculty active on campus at hundreds of universities, colleges and schools of nursing in the United States of America, and a member movement of the International Fellowship of Evangelical Students. For information about local and regional activities, visit intervarsity.org.

All Scripture quotations, unless otherwise indicated, are taken from THE HOLY BIBLE, NEW INTERNATIONAL VERSION®, NIV® *Copyright © 1973, 1978, 1984, 2011 by Biblica, Inc.™ Used by permission. All rights reserved worldwide.*

While any stories in this book are true, some names and identifying information may have been changed to protect the privacy of individuals.

Cover design: Cindy Kiple
Interior design: Beth McGill
Images: red coffee mugs: © SensorSpot/iStockphoto
*   cup of coffee: © s-cphoto/iStockphoto*

ISBN 978-0-8308-4316-9 (print)
ISBN 978-0-8308-9765-0 (digital)

Printed in the United States of America ∞

Library of Congress Cataloging-in-Publication Data
Crabb, Rachael.
  Listen in : building faith and friendship through conversations that matter / Rachael Crabb, Sonya Reeder, and Diana Calvin ; foreword and afterword by Larry Crabb.
    pages cm
  ISBN 978-0-8308-4316-9 (pbk. : alk. paper)
  1. Oral communication—Religious aspects—Christianity. 2. Listening—Religious aspects—Christianity. 3. Female friendship—Religious aspects—Christianity. 4. Interpersonal relations—Religious aspects—Christianity. I. Title.
  BV4597.53.C64C73 2015
  241'.672—dc23

                                                              2014044448

P	21	20	19	18	17	16	15	14	13	12	11	10	9	8	7	6	5	4	3	2	1
Y	32	31	30	29	28	27	26	25	24	23	22	21	20	19	18	17	16	15			

Rachael

to Kimmie and Leslie, my daughters-in-law;

and to Josie, Kaitlyn, Keira and Kensington,

my granddaughters

Sonya

to Abigail, with hope

Diana

to Emily

Sonya, Diana, Rachael

Contents

Foreword

Larry Crabb

S cience and Scripture agree: we are all wired to connect, not just physically with touch but relationally with words. The question is, how can we use words to connect with each other in ways that can do deep and lasting good?

We all live with emotional scars from childhood. Things that happened to you years ago as a little girl have the power to shape how you feel about yourself today and, perhaps more importantly, how you relate to others now as an adult woman. Every woman (and every man) has heard death words spoken to them. Proverbs 18:21 makes it clear that life and death are in the power of the tongue. And, as the book you are about to read will show, life words can weaken the power of death words.

A father sees his young daughter crying and, feeling impatient, says, "You haven't made your bed yet. Stop crying and get busy. It's almost time for school." Lesson learned: she's not worth exploring. She feels invisible. Better to hide who she is than to risk rejection.

Conversations have the power to free women from the ongoing influence of death words, to free you to become the woman God designed you to be. It's true that women, more than men, tend to speak with each other about personal matters. It's also true that opening yourself to other women can be risky. Your authenticity about struggles could stir an urge in a friend to fix you rather than wanting to know you. And that can leave you feeling missed, unseen and alone.

If you recognize that words spoken to you long ago can influence how you feel about yourself today, if you are open to the idea that connecting with other women in good conversations can lessen the controlling power of fear or shame, and if from experience you realize that conversations with the best of intentions can end up doing little good and much harm, then *Listen In* could be life-changing for you.

I admit to some prejudice in favor of the book. I'm married to one of the authors. But as both a man and as a psychologist who has spoken with countless women about what's really going on in their lives beneath the surface, I believe that what you need to hear and understand to live fully alive as a woman lies within these pages.

This is a one-of-a-kind book. You're invited to listen in as these women speak with rare courage and rich wisdom about how wounds from the past can, through the power of Jesus, be transformed into opportunities to relate well today.

Read the book slowly. Digest its message. Share it with your women friends. Get together with them to discuss what you're hearing as you listen in to candid conversations about faith and femininity. Rachael, Sonya and Diana are leading the way for women to engage in a new level of conversations, conversations that powerfully reach into deep hurts and even deeper possibilities. You will not only develop a vision of what it looks like for life words to overcome the power of death words, you will also learn principles to follow that can transform your small group into life-transforming community.

This is a great book, unique in its format, vital in its message. It can change the way you "do conversations" with other women.

Introduction

Three Voices, One Song

Every woman longs to be heard, seen and fully known by other women. One of the best ways to encourage this kind of discovery is through conversations that matter. As a woman reveals her story in all its complexity and is received in ways that reflect the Father's grace and love, she opens herself to the work of the Spirit, who longs to redeem her sin and release her uniquely feminine beauty.

Allow me—Rachael—to introduce you to two of my friends who have experienced the power of real talk among real women. The three of us wanted this project to come from live conversations—nothing scripted—that offer an opportunity to listen in on three women who, despite their daily struggles, want to know God deeply. We know that the kind of conversations that we model in this book can help us to love God more and love each other in new, better ways.

I met Sonya Reeder and her husband, David, when she was a student in Larry's counseling program. In class Sonya sat in the back and seemed to hope no one would notice her.

Outside of class, however, she sought me out as a mentor. Our twenty-year age difference melts away when we are together, and we still see each other every year at our friend Joanie's ranch in Texas.

SONYA WRITES

I'm with other women a lot, counseling and speaking, and through the years I've seen them struggle to know what it means to be a lovely woman for the glory of God. I wrestle with that issue myself. What books can I give women to point them in a direction beyond their own longings and desires? I want us to speak about brokenness and repentance, words that don't often make it into women's books. We can't give our readers any easy answers about how to be lovely or how to be a woman, because we're stumbling along ourselves. But we can talk about finding God in the midst of wrestling with these questions.

I want to have the kind of conversations in which I invite other women to truly see me and to speak into my life with truth and love, not fluff. I want my friends to see me at my very worst and still love me, and I know other women want that too. I think community and good conversations are so essential to finding God. I want people to see me, and I want to see them, in ways that somehow encourage us all to want more of Christ.

Larry and I met Diana Calvin when we served together in Russia on a team to encourage missionaries. Of the younger ones in the group, I immediately recognized Diana as a real sharpie. Our closer contact with her came a few years ago when she attended Larry's School of Spiritual Direction. Since then, we have kept in touch and have come to know her husband, John, and daughter, Emily, as well.

DIANA WRITES

When I talk with women about what is really on their hearts, I am amazed at the beauty that surfaces. There is something stunning about a woman who lets down her guard. So why are these conversations so rare? Why do we struggle, even among the closest of friends, with the temptation to pretend or dramatize or hide or push away?

I want to explore the possibilities for what could happen when a conversation becomes real and women reveal what is truest about themselves. I think that's where we would most clearly see the presence of Christ in us and in one another, and where our small stories could most clearly be seen in light of God's bigger story.

RACHAEL WRITES

As the older woman here, I (Rachael) am interested in writing this book to show how events in our past shape our whole lives as women. I hope that others can hear our discussions and feel encouraged to tell their own stories as well. Proverbs 18:21 tells us that death and life are in the power of the tongue. I want women to see the power that words can have for good or bad as we have conversations that matter. I want us to talk about—and encourage other women to talk about—the most important thing in our lives, and that should be to bring glory to Jesus Christ.

We're three distinct and different voices coming together to sing in harmony and talk about what it means to be a woman of beauty. And we invite you to *listen in*. We hope that even as you hear voices that are a bit off-tune or out-of-sync, you'll recognize the common melody in a song that every woman longs to sing.

WHY *LISTEN IN* IS IN DIALOGUE FORM

We want our readers to join in our conversation, and we want you to start your own conversations with *your* friends. We want you to relate to us as women who also struggle, and who long for your beauty to be discovered and revealed. Together, we can move toward becoming women who talk with one another in ways that help us live for kingdom purposes instead of our self-serving desires and agendas.

We invite you to enter into the conversation and read between the lines for yourself. Ponder what is stirred in you as you hear our words. Imagine yourself as a fourth participant: What questions are you asking? What are you feeling? What do you want? Look for the movement that is there, and explore how your own conversations are either similar to or different from ours. Consider how our dialogues help you see more clearly what you want to give and to receive in a conversation.

Are you up for the challenge? We promise it will be worth the work, the risk, the thought and the involvement required. As a result of your investment, you may find yourself and good friends moving into conversations that will profoundly impact your journey. Imagine conversations that draw you into deeper relationships that lovingly stir repentance, that open doors to experiencing more of God's mercy and grace, and that awaken you to the thrilling awareness of the beauty his amazing grace has already placed deep in your being.

After talking together for more hours than we can count, and asking for Larry's input, we've discerned five key ingredients that, when combined, produce good conversation, *conversation that matters*.

FIVE KEY INGREDIENTS

As you listen in, look for these ingredients and use the questions to help you navigate our discussions. Then let these questions guide you in conversations of your own with close friends who share your desire to have a conversation that matters for the kingdom of God.

Ingredient 1: Identify an intentional purpose. What do I want more than anything to result from this conversation? What might get in the way of pursuing that purpose?

Good conversations develop when each participant is able to articulate and agree on a common goal or purpose that everyone wants to realize. The purpose of uniquely Christian conversations is to discover and cooperate with how the Spirit is working to make us fully alive as women for God's delight, for the blessing of others and for our deepest joy.

Ingredient 2: Tune in to present experience. What am I feeling, thinking and struggling with as I listen in to this conversation? How engaged am I in what is being said?

Authentic relating can only happen when each participant commits herself to paying close attention to what is going on internally, "in the moment," asking: What am I feeling right now? What am I struggling with right now? What am I thinking right now, in the immediate moment of this conversation? What am I holding back? What do I wish I had the courage to share? How am I right now being influenced by others, and how am I influencing them?

Ingredient 3: Be curious and offer feedback. Do I genuinely want to know what this person is thinking and feeling, or am I trying to make a particular point? What words can I offer this person to let her know the hope of the gospel in redeeming her story?

Soul-to-soul conversations happen when each participant is more eager to know what's happening in another (sacred curiosity) than to make a point to another. No "fixing" allowed. Flow with genuine, gentle curiosity. Soul-to-soul nourishment develops when what is most alive in one person (in response to what is happening in the conversation) is warmly and wisely offered to another: "As I hear you say that, this is what stirs in me as I envision where God is leading you."

Ingredient 4: Explore shaping events. What painful events have defined "death" incorrectly for this person? What affirming events have defined "life" incorrectly for her? What selfish goals is she living for as a result of these wrong definitions?

Our history shapes us. Our destiny reshapes us. Painful events (rejection, abuse and shame) in our past lead us to define death *as the recurrence of similar events and associated painful emotions. Pleasant events (affirmation, success and acceptance) lead us to define* life *as the recurrence of similar events that trigger satisfying emotions. We therefore live for no higher purpose than to avoid death (wrongly defined) and to gain life (wrongly defined). But we most often do not see the selfish goals we're living for. Transforming conversations include tearful, joyful discussion of what has happened in the past that is shaping how we relate and what we pursue in the present.*

Ingredient 5: Create a vision. What is visible right now in this person that reflects God's character and beauty? What could become visible in how she relates that would reveal the life of Jesus in uniquely feminine form?

Hopeful conversations focus on what is presently visible in another's life that reflects God's character and beauty, and on what could become visible in how a woman relates that would reveal the life of Jesus in uniquely feminine form. For example, "I see such tenderness coming out of you as we are talking. I feel it and enjoy it. And I get excited when I imagine how the beauty of noncontrolling tenderness could pour out of you even more."

1

Hands over My Mouth

Rachael's Story

Rachael second from left.

THE DAY I LOST MY VOICE

Picture a two-and-a-half-year-old girl alive with excitement and fear. Her mother has been gone for an eternity in her mind and is now coming home. Wiggling and squirming with excitement and chattering to her older sisters. *I want nothing more than to be seen, heard and acknowledged as Mommy's little girl.*

Now, picture a row house with an entry vestibule, like a mudroom, and an umbrella stand in the corner. The upper half of the door is glass with no curtains. At night I never wanted to be in that entry. I was scared that everyone could see all the way into the house. A second interior door, with a sheer curtained upper half, led to the long hallway running alongside the living room. At the end of that hallway are stairs to the second floor, where mother and baby Lowell were to be carried to the nursery.

Mother had left for the hospital two weeks before to deliver Lowell, and he was one of two newborns to survive a staph infection that took the lives of seventeen other babies. I didn't know any of this; all I knew was that I missed my mother. And now they were coming home!

The ambulance arrived quietly at our home, but I did not see it. I was not peering out the living room window onto the street, nor was I standing on the porch to watch my mother and baby brother arrive on a stretcher. Instead my ten- and fourteen-year-old sisters, who were making sure I was out of the way, sat waiting on the dining room table (yes, *on* the table) with one on either side of me.

I heard the front door open, and I could not wait to see Mother! At first I could not see her, but as they brought her down the hallway to the stairs, she came into view. I could hardly sit still, and I yelled out, "Mother, Mother!" Immediately two hands covered my mouth, and my sisters said, "Quiet! The baby is sleeping." It was as if they had put a pin in my party balloon.

I wish my sisters would have held me on their laps or acknowledged that I was excited. Instead, that day they covered my mouth and silenced me. That day I lost my voice, and for years to come I stayed silent. This single event began to shape my life, my journey, and began to incorrectly define who I would become.

STAYING ON THE SURFACE

Thursday evening at Joanie's ranch

Rachael   Before we began, you, Sonya, asked how I was
               feeling starting this conversation about losing my

voice. You noted that losing my voice was the catalyst to the rest of my story. That incident with my sisters that I shared with you set me up for everything that has affected me in a negative way, yet right now I do not have a fear of talking because I can tend to stay on the surface. My comfort zone is to tell a story about someone else in detail before sharing the depths of me. But I don't mind being pulled back from the surface when I trust the hearts behind the questions.

Diana So are you uncomfortable about where we might take you?

Rachael No, excited. I've known each of you for some time, in different ways. So I think I'm excited for where we're going to go with this conversation.

Sonya I wonder what it is like for you to tell that story now.

Rachael Until we started this whole process, I never even thought of this story. Writing this memory gave me the opportunity to call my sisters and ask what they recalled about the night Lowell came home. They each told the story I remembered, but added things I never remembered, like Daddy directing traffic in the hallway, moving the metal coat rack in order to get the stretcher moved up the stairs. Neither sister could recall where my older brother, Philip, was during the confusion. And they didn't remember putting their hands over my mouth. One said, "I don't remember doing it, but I can picture that we did."

Sonya Was your dad excited about your mom coming home, and if so how did he show it?

Rachael	Oh, yeah! I'm sure he was. But they were bringing home a very sick baby, and he never showed emotions. That was part of his generation.
Diana	But you were very excited?
Rachael	Yes, to see Mother! My sisters inadvertently squelched my excitement when they put their hands over my mouth. I lost my voice when they did that. Getting excited was not something I felt free to do. As I got older, whenever I got excited my daddy's phrase was, "Don't jump off the water tower."
Diana	What did "jump off the water tower" mean? Impulsive?
Rachael	Yes, jumping into things without thinking.
Sonya	Do you ever remember a time when your dad just loved that part of you?
Rachael	Oh no! Oh *(laughing)* no. Oh my goodness no! No! No!
Sonya	How about your mother?
Rachael	Oh, she just was umm *(makes a level hand motion)*.
Sonya	Does that mean kind of flatlined?
Rachael	Mother had few ups and downs. I really got to know my folks when they moved to Florida to be close to us. We recorded them having a Q&A with our family. The last question Larry asked each of them was their favorite Bible verse. Mother's was from 1 Timothy 6:6, "Godliness with contentment is great gain." Larry hit me on the knee and whispered so Mother couldn't hear, "Now I know why your mother is so flatlined. That verse is her image of herself. That verse is her ideal."

Sonya	So, you must have really concerned your folks. It seems your dad thought girls should be gentle and quiet, and your mother thought contented. How did you fall on *that* continuum?
Rachael	I was not *on* the continuum.
Sonya	How about your siblings? Were they on the continuum?
Rachael	Yes, they were right on line, very studious, very accomplished.
Diana	So, when you came along you really kind of broke the mold?
Rachael	Yes, noisy, outgoing, trying desperately to be heard.
Sonya	Today, if we said to somebody who knows you, "Early in life, Rachael lost her voice," would most of them say, "Really?" Would they be surprised?
Rachael	The "always have something to say party waiting to happen" mask has been in place for a long time. Until a few years ago I felt, and it was reinforced to me, that I had no substance. My family called me "Sweet Petunia," and they saw me as the helpless little posy, nice to look at but no one to know.
Sonya	What were you thinking in your internal world?
Rachael	I didn't know there was an internal part to offer. No one in my family ever thought about the internal world. At least not out loud.
Sonya	Do you feel like you have substance to offer Diana and me? How about to others? Have you always felt you had substance to offer?
Rachael	Yes, to you and Diana. No to always! I almost wonder

if it didn't shift with the death of my parents. Daddy passed away seventeen years ago at the age of ninety-two, and Mother "went to be with the Lord" (as I was brought up to say when a Christian died) at age ninety-seven, right before we started this project. With them gone maybe I was released to acknowledge things I couldn't say with them here.

Diana   I wonder how many women feel released when their parents die? That's really a shame.

Rachael   It really is. My parents were such good people, but like so many of us moms and dads, they never really tried to know their kids, at least not me.

Sonya   That's very sad, and I'll bet very common. But can I go back a minute to something else? Who called you Sweet Petunia?

Rachael   My siblings, never my parents. My folks were very respectful; I was always Rachael. One day Daddy said something that surprised me about my name. When we lived in Boca Raton, I introduced my parents to a friend at church. The friend asked, "Which one of you does she take after?" My parents kind of looked around the room as if to blame me on someone else, but my father whipped around and said, "Uh, she's her own person. We named her Rachael Joy because she's the joy of our lives." I was stunned to hear that.

Diana   You *never* heard that before?

Rachael   I'd never heard that I was the joy of their lives.

Sonya   And did he say it with delight?

Rachael   You know, it was just an interaction of sweetness that

I observed, even standing off to the side. Bill (my friend) said that he thought I was a joy too.

Sonya So, what did *you* grow up believing about yourself?

Rachael I talk too much, I am too outspoken and no one listens.

Sonya Maybe you felt you had to be gregarious and outspoken to be heard.

Rachael Yes, but now I want my voice to have substance on behalf of another person.

Diana Giving your voice for the sake of another?

Rachael Yes, for them. And that deep shift is very difficult after age sixty, but I'm willing to change. I mentioned to you before that I've been with a group of women for twenty years, and they actually listen to me. When they look at me as I talk, I get so nervous I don't know what to say, but I do recognize that I've got a voice to give on their behalf.

Sonya I have a follow-up question, Rachael, but it is late. I know I am tired and can imagine you are as well. How about we call it a night and pick this up tomorrow morning?

Rachael Good idea.

REFLECTING ON MY EXPERIENCE: RACHAEL

Sonya encouraged me with the reflection that she has noticed a change in me in the area of surface sharing since we've been doing this project. My thoughts are that we have all made changes. Soulful conversations will afford that; they invite change. The intentional purpose of exploring my story was to get an understanding of the events that closed my mouth, and begin to understand the deep change that this conversation was enabling.

I know I have gone deeper, though I realize I still prefer surface conversations. So I decided to trust my friends to explore with me the shaping events and ramifications of my story.

My friends seemed shocked at the nickname "Sweet Petunia" and were curious to know if there was more to it than a term of supposed endearment. They wanted to understand what was going on inside of me, in my internal world as I shared. My honest response was I didn't know there was an internal part to offer. A conversation that matters will enable the participants to dive underneath what is being said to what is meant, to what is hidden—perhaps even to the speaker. God was rewriting the false belief that I had nothing to offer, but I would not have known that had I not allowed my friends to share their vision for me, which was allowing the deepest part of my soul to be known and heard.

When being assured that I offer substance and have been offering substance during this project, I began to realize that there is a transformation taking place inside of me. I do have a voice! I am not just a storyteller or an entertainer. Sharing these feelings with Sonya and Diana turned into a conversation about what kind of voice is coming alive in me.

A SECRET REVEALED

Friday morning at Joanie's ranch

Sonya   Rachael, when we broke off our conversation last night, you were saying you now recognize you have a voice to give. Has giving that voice affected your relationship with Larry?

Rachael   Yes! I will give you an example. Larry is often working on writing a book, and as he completes each chapter he reads it to me, and I usually just say, "That's good." But one evening he was reading the Galatians chapter from *66 Love Letters*, highlighting love throughout the book. When he finished, I said, "I can't think of one love verse in the book of Galatians." Instead of my usual two-word responses, I begin to dialogue with him about this. He became so excited. We went on for the next half hour, looking up verses, reading commentaries and continuing the conversation.

Sonya   I wish I could have seen Larry's face!

Rachael   Oh, not just his face! He was so animated (and surprised) that I was offering my voice for his sake.

Diana   Wow, what an amazing change for you and Larry. It makes me wonder, though, why you kept talking as a child. If no one noticed you or listened to you, why didn't you just shut down?

Rachael   There is talking to talk, and then there is not talking and calling it losing your voice. I think I was talking to see if anyone heard me, and I did not like lulls.

Diana   You're tearing up.

Rachael   I think you hit my core terror—I'm all alone and no one is around to see me, hear me or protect me.

Diana   How does the thought of being alone connect to such great fear?

Rachael   From ages eight to twelve I was abused by a neighbor, and I felt I couldn't tell anyone. If I did, would they listen? I have nightmares and mouth herpes to this day. It took me eighteen years of marriage to even tell my husband.

Diana   Sounds like that part of you convinced yourself that
          you had no voice, really scared you to death as it
          allowed the abuse to continue.

Rachael   The abuse continued because of my being convinced
          I had no voice. I realized that I have kept talking—
          talking to talk. My modus operandi insulated me
          from need, insulated me from needing to be pro-
          tected because I was convinced that no one would
          protect me. By keeping busy inside and out, I did not
          have to deal with the truth that though I had words,
          I truly had no voice. Not a voice that mattered. But
          thankfully that's changing. Larry says his vision for
          me is that I would rest, truly rest. A part of that rest
          is living out of the internal voice that God has given
          me, the voice of substance.

Diana   This is how it sounds to me: when your mom died,
          somehow you got permission to look at and deal
          with what had been covered up for over fifty years.
          You don't feel like you only have to entertain. Your
          depth and true substance comes out and blesses us.

Rachael   Thank you! I would never have done this if we
          weren't having these conversations.

Sonya   I think the timing of it is all God. We slid in right after
          your mother died. And you've been nothing but
          open with us, Rach. Sometimes you go off on those
          rabbit trail stories about someone else, but when we
          pull you back, you don't stiff-arm or fight us.

Diana   How did you receive what we just said to you?

Rachael   Grateful. Grateful to have gals in my life who I be-
          lieve speak the truth. I still have a problem with ac-

colades that are not truthful. I've been speaking for over thirty years, and as people leave they have often said, "Oh, you are so refreshing." I told Larry that if I hear one more person say that I'm refreshing, I'm going to slap them. (*laughter*) I believe they mean the party was happening here with me as the speaker, all fun, no substance. I am pleased to report that people do not say that as much as they used to.

Diana   Really? Have you changed as a speaker?

Rachael   My personality hasn't changed, so before I speak I remind God that he made me this way and I will use my outgoing temperament for him. I want to have some depth, truth and wisdom imparted from him through me to the audience.

Sonya   Yeah, you're sitting here joking about "refreshing" being a bad thing and I'm kind of going, *Rachael, you are refreshing and it's a good thing!*

Rachael   But being called "refreshing" hurt my feelings and tender heart. It's what was always said about me. "Oh, here comes Rachael; the party's going to begin. Oh, she's so fun loving, you will just have a ball. If you play tennis with Rachael, you might not win on her team but you will have the best time." That's how I hear "refreshing."

Sonya   But if I said to you what you offer me is refreshing . . .

Rachael   I'd take it from you differently because I know the heart behind it. With people who come up to me after I speak, I don't know the heart behind their words.

Diana   You know it takes more than fluff to refresh Sonya.

Rachael   That's right. It's good from her.

Diana   I believe you are becoming very aware that you have
           depth and substance to give to others. I hope you
           never quit offering who you really are. I love that.
           There is so much more, beyond fun, to you that
           people have not gotten to see. And from your story
           I believe some of them have really missed seeing the
           real you.

Rachael   Yes! You can have fun. I'm always thinking of all the
           fun stuff to do for people, but it isn't my whole
           identity. If I'm not the party, I can accept that.

Sonya   Tell me this: How have you repented?

Rachael   How have I repented? That's a shift. But maybe a
           good one! Are you saying that my refusal to have a
           voice for Christ is a form of relational sin? I think
           you are saying that, and I think you're right.

Sonya   You're putting it better than I could have, but, yes,
           that's what I was thinking.

Rachael   It's a daily act of repentance. It's really hard for me
           to not take charge of making the fun and getting the
           accolades. It's not bad to make the fun, but it is sin
           to use the fun to avoid giving myself.

Sonya   And when you don't take charge of the parties, do you
           feel lost?

Rachael   At first, I did feel lost. It was awkward. But people
           began to get used to me not being the party giver.
           The different responses I got from friends were
           funny. One friend used to say, "I wonder what
           favors Rachael brought in her suitcase for us at
           this meal." Some "friends" have gotten angry
           when I didn't bring the party. This has shown me

the differences in people's hearts. Some are accepting, and some expecting. This was and often still is my identity.

Scripture calls hospitality one of the gifts. It has to do with brotherly love and doing it more for Christ and not for me.

Sonya How does the scriptural definition of hospitality play out in you?

Rachael I did not and do not want to come solely from the place of entertainment. I want to be known as a woman of substance that gives with a hospitable heart. I remember one day being in a small group of authors who were excited to have dinner in our home. One in particular would come in and say, "We have the most fun with you as a hostess." And I said, "Well, I'm the only author in this room who wrote a book on hospitality, you know." Ha ha ha! That is how I would pass it off, but that touched something very deep in me, and it showed me how cemented my identity was in that group.

Diana Where does repentance come in?

Rachael Daily repentance, recognizing the sinful self-protection in my being the "party waiting to happen" is needed. It's what I want to continue to be about. It is all a part of God's redeeming work.

Sonya What's the redeemed part look like?

Rachael The redeemed part is giving what is deepest within me out of a well of forgiveness, giving what is beautiful and loving at whatever cost to me. I've got to be forgiving toward people who don't affirm my substance, not demanding that they do and then losing my voice because they might not.

REFLECTING ON MY EXPERIENCE: RACHAEL

The room grew quiet as Diana and Sonya digested what I had just shared with them. Losing my voice had allowed a crime against my innocence. My "life of the party" mask held a secret that was silenced along with my internal voice. I believe each of us hides a core terror. This core terror is something we share with few people, because we are convinced if they really understood who we are at our depth, we would experience rejection or further pain. A conversation that truly matters can be a catalyst that dispels long-held beliefs that are not true. Diana's feedback centered on the timing of this project and finding my true inner voice.

A conversation that matters can put pieces of an intricate life puzzle together in a way that brings revelation and growth. Shaping events are often best understood by being afforded the opportunity to sit back and get a fresh perspective on them. Those events, when understood, spark a fresh vision for life.

Learning to Listen In

For Reflection or Small Group Discussion

Ingredient 1. Identify an Intentional Purpose

Rachael's life-defining moment was when her sisters put their hands over her mouth. That day she was told to not talk, and the result was that she lost her voice for many years. The purpose of the conversation was to understand the dynamics of Rachael's story and how her identity was shaped. Meaningful conversations have Holy Spirit–led agendas.

- What kingdom purposes can be achieved by having conversations that are intentional?

Ingredient 2. Tune In to Present Experience

Rachael's core terror was (is) being alone in a crowded room with no one to hear her voice. Look at the picture. She is a tiny child surrounded by towering siblings who did not see her, hear her, nor protect her.

- What are some ways that people protect themselves?

- How do you keep people from getting to the real you, the inner-beautiful real you?

Ingredient 3. Be Curious and Offer Feedback

Rachael came to understand herself and her story more by sharing it with Sonya and Diana. At one point Sonya becomes curious and makes the statement that she will always ask questions to draw Rachael back into the depths of herself that others need to experience. When you are listening to another's story, what are some questions that you can use to begin a deeper dialogue? Here are two questions to get you started:

- What is a word that you would use to describe yourself?
- What do you remember as the "worst day of your life"? Or, what comes to mind as the "best day of your life"?

Ingredient 4. Explore Shaping Events

Rachael was willing to dig deep beneath her identity to discover the lies and wounds that defined it. She was willing to let God redefine accurately who she is.

- Who has written the foundation of your identity?
- The events of Rachael's life stripped her of true soul rest. What is a definition of a woman at rest? What does she look like, act like? How does she think?

Ingredient 5. Create a Vision

Proverbs instructs that death and life are in the power of the tongue. "Sweet Petunia" was a death thought for Rachael. A death word can be an action, a phrase, an attitude toward you that incorrectly defines who you are. Rachael did not know that a petunia is a strong flower; she did not know that she had substance. In Rachael's mind, even as a child, "Sweet Petunia" meant she had no substance, no depth. She was to be a mascot, present but not heard. Rachael's death word was redeemed as a life word when looked at through the grid of God's Word and a community of like-minded friends who want to be known, discovered and explored. Her friends were giving her a vision of how God had truly designed her to be.

- Discuss your "death words" and discover in meaningful conversation how God has redeemed, or can redeem, your death words with his life words.

2

Finding My Voice

Rachael's Response

SPEAKING WITH A NEW ENERGY

Sixty years suffering under the control of my death word is entirely too long. I long for women to be much sooner set free from the controlling death actions or words that have kept them in bondage. I love talking to high school girls at a local Christian school in an elective course on being a godly woman. I talk about death and life words, praying that perhaps they will be freed to live out their life words. Recently, I watched as a girl shared, with tears, her death word: *noisy*. I then asked her peers who knew her to take a few minutes and picture her in the center of the triune God and "listen" to the three persons as they talked about her. We came back together and the girls told affirming stories about her. But it was the teacher who spoke powerful words of life: "Kay, you were on the debate team last year, and your passion cheered everyone on to that state championship. I'd say that you're not noisy, you are passionate." Kay wiped tears from her eyes and a smile came over her face. Several weeks later I received a letter from a girl in the class. She started it by saying, "Dear Mrs. Crabb, my name is Heather and I sat

next to Kay (the girl who cried). Thank you for helping us recognize that we don't have to live our lives with death words
controlling us." I thought to myself, *That's what I want for women
to have, release from death words.*

During my sixty years I erected a wall around me. I wrote a
book on hospitality, was called a "party waiting to happen" and
was known as "refreshing," someone with a good personality, but
I stayed on the surface because revealing too much about what
was going on inside me was too risky. In my early sixties Sonya,
Diana and I decided to write this book, and, to tell the truth, I
wasn't excited about sharing deeply with anyone. However, they
wanted to have redeeming conversations that mattered. That
meant I would have to talk about specifics in my life, especially
in my internal world. Yikes! It's so much easier to talk about the
specifics, even minute details, of a friend, but writing this book
meant I could no longer hide behind another's story but would
have to reflect on my own. So the journey began into acknowl-
edging that I had been controlled by something said to me. I
became excited about the discovery of what my ruling passion
was: talk to talk, entertain as a storyteller and stay on the surface.

I hid my fear of revealing myself by judging others. I often
approached people without loving energy or even a vision about
who that person could be if Christ got ahold of her (and me).
The energy in my voice and actions was edgy. I will relate a story
to illustrate my point. The church we attended hired a new
Christian education pastor, and I had to make an appointment
to see him. Here's why. Before the new Christian education
pastor was hired, John, a good friend, and I had voluntarily
headed up the Sunday school program through the eighth grade.
We arranged a whole rotation of teachers and substitutes, and
found unused materials to use, which substantially helped with

the church budget. Everything was finally going smoothly in an area that had previously been in shambles. But the new pastor threw John and me under the bus and hired a person to take *our* "job." John and I felt blindsided. Since John's work for a large corporation in town limited his time, I knew I would have to be the one to chat with the pastor. I went in with the urge of justice and never once had a vision for this guy or thought that he might be living out of his own death word, perhaps trying to prove himself at our expense. My energy was bad and my hurt hit his fear—not pretty. I was living out my self-protective agenda to talk, talk to be heard, to get justice. In no way was I beautifully invitational.

I have many shameful memories of not relating with the energy of Christ, which could have been powerfully working in me (Colossians 1:29). At times I still fall back into self-protection. But, because I now have a category of understanding that goes through my mind before I speak (am I relating to this person or event with a vision for them, and am I relating to them as the Trinity relates?), I can speak authentically with the energy of Christ in me. And that is relational holiness, valuing the other more highly than myself.

Since working on this book with Sonya and Diana, I have found my true voice. And it's making a difference. For example, I have known Janie for twenty-five years, but have not seen her in person in two years. I Skype with her on a monthly basis, and last week during a Skype call she made a statement that put a song in my heart and a smile on my face. She told me that she loves our times together and can't wait to see me in person, soon! She then went on to say that she wants to tell me how I come across to her. I was all ears because I felt our relationship could handle anything. She said that I was much more relaxed and

authentic than she has ever known me to be. Yes! She "saw" the
energy of Christ in me, and her soul was encouraged to become
more fully alive as a woman. That is what I trust this chapter
encourages you to reflect on as you read our conversation. "The
tongue has the power of life and death" (Proverbs 18:21).

DIRECTING THE UNIVERSE

Sunday afternoon at Joanie's ranch

Rachael   This is our conversation on outspokenness versus . . .
we'll just go with outspokenness and see what the
"versus" is. We have been discovering how I lost my
voice and exploring the shaping events that resulted
in protecting and hiding my core self. And right
now I am feeling a little outspoken! I don't know if
it's good outspokenness or a bad outspokenness. I
am defining and identifying words based on my
story. It's all about me, and this makes me feel outspoken. When I hear the word *outspoken*, the first
thing that comes to mind is negative, but the redemption side of being outspoken is what I hope
we unpack. Sonya once mentioned that when
someone is referred to as being outspoken it usually
is not a compliment or a term of endearment! So,
ladies, let's talk about being outspoken!

Diana   Well, let me say this, I don't think anybody's ever
said to me "you're outspoken," but I would not be
surprised if someone has said behind my back
"she's outspoken." So, I think it's something so
negative that people don't say it to your face, just
behind your back.

Rachael	Well, I had "she talks too much" written on report cards, which is very similar to outspoken!
Diana	People might use words like *opinionated* . . .
Sonya	Or, *She says what she thinks.*
Diana	Yeah, *She's blunt.* But it's all the same thing, and usually said when the object of the conversation is not around.
Sonya	It is really all negative.
Rachael	What would it look like if it were positive? We wouldn't use the word *outspoken* if it were positive, would we?
Sonya	Well, I think of you as outspoken.
Rachael	*(chuckle)* Oh good! Oh *good*!
Diana	In a good way!
Rachael	And what does *that* mean?
Sonya	Well, I think when you, Rachael, have something on your heart to say, you say it. I've only known you for twenty-four years, so I don't know what it was like forty years ago, but I believe that when you speak your heart, you do so with directness and kindness.
Diana	You know, when you say things to people, you're not saying it through the back door. For example, "Well, do you think maybe, kinda, you might want to think about . . ." No, you're very direct.
Sonya	You have done that with friends when you've seen husbands or wives in certain situations and you have taken them to the side. Sometimes I think outspokenness is being willing to take a stand for the sake of love—being willing "to go out on a limb" for the sake of another person.

Rachael	Oh, now that sounds really nice.
Diana	Better than *opinionated* and *blunt.*
Rachael	It does!
Sonya	Sometimes the reference has been "a bulldog." Have you ever heard that one?
Rachael	Yes, and I have had people tell me, "You know, when I got home I realized you really told me off, but I did not know it at the time." I have had Andi say to me, "You told me off in such a nice way I did not take offense." I don't think that is being too straight-forward, nor would I call it outspoken.
Diana	She knows that you are "for her," so you can say things to her that are very outspoken, very clear, and she appreciates it.
Rachael	Uh huh. And I wonder, do I appreciate it when people say things to me? Maybe it *is* the tone of voice and the attitude in which they say it that causes me to react one way or the other.
Diana	The mood behind it?
Rachael	The heart behind it.
Diana	And for the sake of the other. That's really the bottom line because, you know, lots of times outspokenness is just being a bitch. I want my way, and I'm gonna tell you all about it, and there's nothing good about that.
Sonya	If you look in Scripture, the women in the Bible were outspoken.
Rachael	And those were times that it was really not socially acceptable.

Sonya	Right! This means they took a risk. And I do think that good outspokenness takes a risk on behalf of another person.
Rachael	So it is very relational.
Diana	For example, in 1 Samuel 25, Abigail didn't act on her own behalf; she actually put herself at great risk to speak up.
Sonya	And I think outspokenness calls something better out of a person, which is what she did with David. She was calling him to be a better man. I think when we are outspoken, as godly Spirit-led women; we are loving the other person. We're calling them to be what God's designed them to be.
Rachael	So in all, it's the heart and agenda behind the words. However, I still picture outspokenness as very negative.
Diana	Well, I think we, as women, have used it negatively in a lot of ways. I know I do. When I want something, my way of being outspoken is to argue. I'm a good arguer. All I have to do, and I can be very nice about it, is line up my points. You know 1, 2, 3 and . . .
Rachael	John can't beat your logic?
Diana	What's he gonna say? And it's not for *him* at all. It's because *I* want my way, and this is the best way I can think of to get it. I have definitely done that.
Rachael	I know that's in all of us. I know how it shows in me, as Larry's nickname for me has always been "Director of the Universe." He says, "Um, there you go again—DU." People around town have heard this story, and it's gotten to the point now that our dentist says, "Here comes the DU." You know, funny things like that, and I know it's not a compliment.

Sonya   For most of my life, I have been hard or not inviting,
         and somewhere along the line I think I've had
         people in my life take those words, *hardness* or *un-
         inviting* and squash my own outspokenness.
         They've used the outspokenness and said, "You
         speak too much, or you do this too much, or you
         ask too many questions, or you do . . ." So I've
         gotten confused between it's okay to be outspoken
         and it's not okay to be . . .

Rachael Outspoken. It's okay to be outspoken but it's not
         okay to be *outspoken*!

Sonya   Yeah.

Diana   Do you have trouble deciding when you're being *hard*
         and *outspoken*? Do you know what I'm saying?

Sonya   I know I do. Several years ago I just didn't say any-
         thing. Then I started going through life kind of
         "disappearing" and keeping inside. And I would just
         get by and would feel a lot of things or I would
         have a lot going through my head. I swung from
         one end of the spectrum to the other. And neither
         one of those are lovely.

Diana   Well, they are both all about you and nothing to do
         with the other person.

Sonya   Right.

Rachael Then you are never at rest inside. You are always
         calculating, *How can I* . . .

Sonya   Yes, always trying to figure it out. But I do think out-
         spokenness can be a good thing and can be a lovely
         thing in a woman.

REFLECTING ON MY EXPERIENCE: RACHAEL

I want conversation that flows from me to come from my inner beauty. A big part of my story is about finding my voice. There's a good way to find my voice, a way that reveals the beauty in me, and there is finding my voice so I'm just talking to talk or be heard, or to control someone, or to "Direct the Universe!"And there's no beauty in that!

A person can be beautiful on the outside and be the ugliest person inside. And a person could be rather ordinary looking on the outside, but when you look at her, she is glowing because she has inner beauty. I want people to read my story and see the beauty that God has granted!

I want to relate in a way that provokes others to think, to reflect, to share. I don't want to push my thoughts on others. My life word is *authentic*. For me, that means being who I am for the sake of others. Too often, my relational style has been to win the response from others that I want and to hear my own voice, which for so many years had been taken from me. But now I long to reflect the incredible relationship among the three divine persons, where each person honors the other. Their way of relating defines the dance of the Trinity. I want to dance into others' lives to their rhythm.

THE BEAUTY IN BEING OUTSPOKEN

Sunday evening at Joanie's ranch

Rachael During our break I have been thinking more intently about the topic of outspokenness. I think this concept is perhaps more complex and intricate than people have understood. Especially for women!

Diana Think about what we say to our children. You know, there's so much a mother can say to children that they can't hear anywhere else. I want to be outspoken with Emily. I don't want to hold back how much I love her, how much I want for her. I want to be clear with her about those things. And I want her to see me as a woman who speaks and gives and doesn't hold back. I want to model that for her.

Rachael But you do it in an authentic way. I think of *authenticity* as "I will be all of who I am, but gentler. You will get all of me when I speak." I will be who I am, yet not with an edge but gentle and inviting.

Diana So why is authentic gentle? Why wouldn't authentic be "Well, this is the *real* me. Take it or leave it!"

Rachael Just like outspokenness. When you are outspoken in a gentle way, I think that is something of who you really are. Deep down, because of the indwelling Holy Spirit, you really are a nice person wanting to come out and help other people, to be for other people.

Diana The Spirit of God through Jesus Christ is there beneath the flesh, beneath the crap.

Rachael Yes. And so often that flesh gets the outspokenness. We speak out of the flesh, not the Spirit.

Diana Yeah.

Rachael So I think there is a difference, and we can know it and do it. All my life I was told I was outspoken. But I know why now. In many ways I was trying to find my voice. I wanted someone to hear me, and the best way was to be outspoken in a loud, obnoxious way.

Diana Just talk all the time.

Rachael	Yeah. I was talking just to be heard. Because I wasn't heard at home, I demanded to be heard at school. And let them put on my report card "She talks too much." It was the same idea. It was negative, and those words affect us in the same way. I became harder and louder and not inviting.
Diana	Yeah.
Sonya	I think we've become outspoken at times because we really want to matter. We think if we're outspoken, we'll matter.
Rachael	Yeah, louder and louder.
Sonya	And then it carries a negative connotation again, as it comes from a sinful place in us. For me to arrange my life to make sure that I matter to you, I'm doing great harm at that point.
Rachael	I like the way you called it "a sinful place," because so many people would say "a wound," and not say what it really is.
Sonya	It can be a wound when you did not matter as a kid. I was always trying to matter as a kid. With that wound and with a clenched fist I demanded "I will matter to you," and it became a deep, sinful place for me.
Diana	It's where you take the wound and how you live out of that place that can become sinful.
Rachael	The bigger problem is the wound. Because you're coming out of hurt, you pick up your fist and declare, "You will hear me!" I might shake you by the shoulders, in my mind, and you will get it.

Diana	"You are going to hear me and you won't hurt me."
Rachael	That's right. "You will hear me, and I will be right. I will be the Director."
Sonya	I think I've spent most of my life like that.
Rachael	That was sort of a posture you presented to us, except yours was the crossed-arm one.
Sonya	Oh, did I? That was the visual. Maybe it was shaking fists by the time I was a bit older.
Rachael	Oh, I'm sure you decided you wouldn't get too open. Keep the fists closed. Keep the heart closed, not open.
Sonya	Yeah.
Diana	So, now that we know what harm we can do with outspokenness, when is outspokenness a blessing to people?
Sonya	When *do* we bless people with our outspokenness?
Diana	Sonya, I think you bless people with your outspokenness when you're talking with someone in your counseling office. Or it doesn't have to be in a counseling office. When you say something that you know people aren't going to like but you say it anyway, not to prove them wrong or to score points with them, but because you know it's true and you believe that it's something that's best for them. It's for their sake. If after they process they come back to you and say, "What you said took me to a different place with God," that is wonderful outspokenness to me.
Rachael	Because it comes right from her heart. She's thinking of the other person.

Sonya Thank you, I feel like that's what God is redeeming. He is not done, of course. Twenty-three years ago, people I sat with, my husband included, would say I came at them like a Mack Truck.

Diana Yeah, I've got the answer for you if you'll just let me get it through your thick skull.

Rachael It has to do with energy behind it, doesn't it?

Sonya Definitely. I want to be able to say things with the other person in mind, not needing them to "get it" for my sake, but I want to listen well to others and have the courage to speak what the Spirit leads me to say.

Diana That is exactly what God does with us. He wants a relationship.

Rachael Yeah, you do know the difference once it comes out.

Diana You do. You can tell, can't you?

Rachael Yes, you see it in their eyes that you've just hurt them badly, and you know immediately that it was a nasty energy in you.

Sonya Do you know the difference when you're speaking? Can you tell when you've been the nasty kind? You're chuckling, Rachael.

Rachael Most of the time, I can. Yeah, I think so. What about you girls?

Diana Here's another angle. It is hard to know because you may say things out of a really risky, courageous place in your heart, and it can make the other person really angry at first. In fact, it often will. But you cannot judge it based solely on the person's response.

Sonya   I know when I'm nasty. It usually happens with David, where I can speak something into his life that he may not like, but I can speak it with a mood of "I'm angry. I'm ticked. And you need to get it right and you're not getting it right." Or I can speak it from a place—and this only happens on occasions—of kindness and for the sake of love even though he might not like hearing it.

Rachael   So, then, you know it came from a good place, with a good motive, and I think that makes a lot of difference.

Sonya   I feel like it's something in my gut that's saying "you need to speak this," and when I do it out of a place of security, I sense there's something good that happens between me and God. You know?

Diana   Well, yeah, our words are less demanding when we are sure of God's love and care, and I don't think I'm very sure of that very often. I think I doubt that all the time, and so if God's not going to take care of me, *I'm* going to take care of me.

Rachael   Right.

Diana   Yeah, but when I really do let God's love affect me, I'm much more willing to risk with other people.

Rachael   One of the criteria I have for whether it's an outspoken and nasty thing or that it's really coming from my heart and gentleness is if I rehearse it too much. If I rehearse what my words are going to be, and I'm not even thinking of having a conversation with God about it, not even relating him to the whole thing, but I'm going to take it on myself. I know then that it is coming out of a nasty place.

Sonya   Well, it can't be authentic if you're going to rehearse it.

Diana   Oh, that's good.

Rachael It can't if I'm playing scenarios in my head all the time as to how this should look, what this conversation should be when I'm ticked at someone. I can do the whole scenario of how to tell them off, how to do snotty little things. . . . (*laughter*) I'm good at that, rehearsing the whole thing in my head. I think, *Why pray about it? I've got it handled.*

Sonya   And what's the authentic side of that?

Rachael The gentle, godly, authentic side would be saying, *I don't want to hurt that person. I don't want to be a meanie to them. I want to bless them.* If I put in the "blessing" side as opposed to the "get even" side, there's a big difference. The redeemed side of outspokenness is gentle, godly authenticity that comes from an internal world focused on glorifying God.

Diana   And talking to God about that helps you get to that place.

Rachael It really does. But when I'm doing my own planning, God says, "I have plans for you, and you aren't including me in them."

Sonya   So, how do we, as women, and I'm not looking for a black-and-white answer, move from being outspoken out of protectiveness, in a nasty sort of way, to being authentic and lovely? How does that happen in your lives?

Diana   I'm really drawn to what Rachael said: by spending time with my heavenly Father. You know, instead of telling the person all the different ways they've hurt me or disappointed me, taking that to God, who sees it in my heart anyway. Admitting to him how I feel, where I'm angry, where I'm guilty, whatever it is. This feels like a good place to start.

Rachael Walking in the Spirit as opposed to in the flesh.

Diana Yeah, and calling out to God in my loneliness.

Rachael Then there's that. We need the alone time. We need the rest time. We need the down time to get in relationship with the Trinity. I have not always been good at down time and rest time. So, therefore, much of the time I have been *outspoken*!

Sonya I think we have to come to see it as sin. We have to see it not as just a personality trait, not just something Mom taught me, not just out of woundedness, but when I look at your face and I've been outspoken, unkind, and I've harmed you, it has to stun me and stop me.

Rachael It does because it wasn't anything that our Father would do. I think this is a good time to call it what it is—relational sin, which is valuing my own personal needs above the needs of others, or just being plain old self-centered. When I search for what the Spirit of God is doing in my life I have to cut through some of the insecurities and fears, a demanding spirit, and more. When I am finally broken over my relational sin, I will discover God's power in my passion to change the world.

Sonya And I don't think I can shift over to being authentic until . . .

Diana Until we recognize the relational sin in our lives.

Sonya That's right.

Rachael	God is in the business of forgiveness of sin, and we don't often think of our attitudes as being sin in a relational way. *Sin* is an unpopular word today!
Sonya	It is easier to say that somebody grew up that way.
Rachael	I keep something as a reminder on my desk that is from the cover of the July-August 2005 issue of *Zion's Fire.* The editor, Marv Rosenthal, identifies sin "not as a mistake, not an error, not a disease, not a fault, not a white lie and not an indiscretion; it is universal in scope, deadly in effect and beyond the cure of any manmade antidote." He believes and I agree that it is the three-letter word "sin." We *don't* believe it and we won't use that word.
Diana	Well, it *only* refers to adultery, robbery, murder, and we don't think of self-centered motives as sin.
Sonya	We're so good at explaining it, justifying it, condoning it; we're not very good at being stopped by it.
Diana	We never get to grace, to speak out of a gracious, pretty place. I think that's another thing. You asked, "What would change this?" I think the more aware I am of my need for grace, the less I'm going to go point out everybody else's problems.
Rachael	Makes you softer already, just saying things like that.
Diana	It does. It truly does.
Sonya	As we receive deeply from his grace, it will have everything to do with the quality of what we have to give out to other people.
Rachael	So to respond to our first phrase in this conversation: outspokenness versus authenticity! I think we have

found the redeeming word! I think that's the re-deemed side of the word *outspoken* that we came to in this conversation—*authentic*, the authenticity that is Spirit controlled and driven from the purpose and intention of glorifying God. When I speak honestly from the heart with the well-being of another foremost in my mind, that is authenticity as God would have it. Godly, Spirit-led "good" authenticity: the good and redeemed version of outspokenness.

REFLECTING ON MY EXPERIENCE: RACHAEL

I love Hannah's story and her song when she gave up her baby, Samuel. She didn't sing when she got pregnant; she sang when she gave him up. Why? I'm a songbird when something good happens to me, but I don't sing when something bad happens. And when Hannah gave up Samuel (see 1 Samuel 1), I would have considered that a bad thing. But she had an idea of the larger story.

Gentle, godly authenticity comes from a deep understanding and connection with the Producer and Director of my story. Hannah knew the Father had said, "My Son's the star, and I'm going to give you a bit part. Play it well!"

That is what I want to do, play my part well for the glory of God. I must remember in my bit part there are other voices, other players with parts similar to mine. If I do not acknowledge them, if I stay in my own self-centered world, I will miss their beauty and the beauty of all of us joining together as one song for his glory.

In the conversation we mentioned relational sin. The flip side of relational sin is trying to live a life of relational holiness, being authentic in attitude and action. If relational sin is valuing myself more highly than another, relational holiness is valuing the well-being of another above myself.

The conversation we had took me from death to life simply by chatting with friends and identifying "authentic" as my life word. I am authentic and have so much more confidence in who I am. Even though I have been a Christian from age twelve, I didn't know who perfect Love was until I switched from death to life in words that let me get a glimpse of being the daughter of the King.

Learning to Listen In

For Reflection or Small Group Discussion

Ingredient 1. Identify an Intentional Purpose

Rachael and her friends came to identify the redeemed side of outspokenness as being authentic, that is, Spirit controlled and driven from the purpose and intention of glorifying God.

- Authentic does not mean simply to speak out what's inside. It means to speak out for the sake of others with the intention that your words pour life into another. How might you identify whether "honest sharing" is self-driven or driven by concern for another?

- What has been the reaction when your "authenticity" has been self-driven sharing?

- Share openly and vulnerably with your group about a time when your "authenticity" was actually unredeemed outspokenness. As you discuss, reflect on what harm was done, and what it might mean to repent of relational sin.

Ingredient 2. Tune In to Present Experience

At one point in the conversation Diana tuned in to what was

going on in her heart. She was becoming self-aware and realizing some personal relational sin.

- How are you tempted to quench the Spirit when conversations have triggered a response in your soul that is conviction from the Holy Spirit?

- Pause for a few moments to think about a time when adding to the subject at hand would have meant confessing something you did not want to own. Soulful, meaningful conversations allow for confession and releasing of the sin that hinders the soul from growth. Meaningful dialogue includes being aware of your own internal reactions and being willing to share them with others.

Ingredient 3. Be Curious and Offer Feedback

Rachael's conversations with her friends included being vulnerable and risking feedback from others that may not have been easy to hear. Being willing to enter into soul conversations with defenses down opens our hearts to what the Spirit may be saying.

- When have you experienced an "aha" moment that changed your soul? Or, if you have not experienced those moments, ask the group to help you identify defenses or walls of protection that keep you from truly hearing the Spirit.

Ingredient 4. Explore Shaping Events

Rachael and her friends use open-ended questions that cannot be answered yes or no. Soul-searching conversations that invite deeper understanding and intimate sharing do not have easy answers or quick responses. Encourage each group member to avoid the simple in search for the soulful. Make a conscious decision to avoid closed questions. Catch yourself and each other in this most common way of communicating. Shaping events are best explored with open-ended questions.

Ingredient 5. Create a Vision

Often a person's self-image can be revealed in the way she tells her story, the verses she chose to live out and the Bible characters she most closely relates to. Abigail was mentioned as a woman who risked speaking out.

- Have each member of your group share who their favorite Bible character is and why. Discuss the good, the bad and the ugly about each one. Be curious regarding the choice of characters; explore what might be beneath the words of the speaker.

- To encourage each person on her journey, be ready to share a vision for the speaker based on her favorite character. Call out in each other what and how God has designed them to be.

3

I'm a Girl and I Like Football

Sonya's Story

LOOKING FOR ANSWERS

I was nine years old and in the front yard of our Cleveland, Tennessee, home playing football by myself. Most little girls ask their parents for dolls and Barbies, but for years I had asked for a football uniform. I loved football and desperately wanted to play. For Christmas that year, my mom reluctantly gave in and bought me an Atlanta Falcons football uniform. It came in a box, and in that box was all I needed to transform myself into a real football player—a white and red helmet, shoulder pads that tied in the front, a bright red jersey, and a pair of clean white pants. On weekend mornings I would wake up and could not wait to put on my uniform. One particular morning I was in my front yard trying to play both offense and defense. I threw the ball in the air, caught it and then tackled myself with the hope of staining my bright white pants.

As I was getting up from the ground after tackling myself, a man on a Harley-Davidson pulled into my driveway. He was tall and slender, and wore a leather jacket and sunglasses. He removed his helmet, and I could see his dark hair, slicked back. I stood staring at this man with a guarded skepticism, wondering why he was walking toward me. I remained still and waited for him to tell me who he was and what he wanted. He held out his hand and said hello, and then introduced himself as Raymond, a pastor at a local church. He said he had stopped to see if I might be interested in attending his church. I had many questions going through my head, but, as was my tendency, I waited to ask those questions.

I have always asked questions, but early on I became aware that my questions bothered people. In fact, I was told more than once that I asked *way* too many questions. So, at nine years old I was reluctant to question a stranger who might have posed a threat to me. I was tentative toward all men, including Raymond. I also worried that my questions might make him angry, and I would feel like a bother to him.

Raymond spent about fifteen minutes throwing the football with me. Then he assured me that a church bus would be on my street around 8:30 on Sunday morning if I wanted to come. Raymond was right, and for the next several months I caught the bus to the church. After several weeks of attending Sunday school, I decided to take a chance and ask the teacher some of my questions about Jesus and his love. Within two weeks she was aggravated with me and my questions. She told me that the next Sunday I was to talk to the pastor instead. I felt like I had done something wrong, that she was finished with me. But I did visit with Raymond, and week after week I sat with him and asked him all my questions in the big, musty-smelling sanctuary.

Although I really can't remember my questions or Raymond's answers, I do remember the mood of grace and tenderness he offered me during our talks.

TRYING TO BE TOUGH

Saturday afternoon at Embassy Suites, Dallas, Texas

Rachael   Sonya, I noticed in your story that you often played by yourself. Tell us a little bit about how you played as a child.

Sonya   I can remember it like it was yesterday. I did play by myself a lot. For nine years I was the only child, until my little brother came along. So it was not unusual for me to be by myself. I grew up pretty much alone, and now, as an adult, I arrange my life so that I don't have to spend a lot of time by myself. I am often with others.

Rachael   Well, you can't spend very much time by yourself when you have three kids and a husband. That would be a little hard. Do you rest?

Sonya   No, I really don't. Resting is hard for me.

Diana   So, was it restful for you as a child to play by yourself? Did you enjoy it?

Sonya   Oh, I loved it. I loved playing. I loved being outside in the front yard with my football uniform and my football. I did not like sitting in the house by myself.

When I was in the house, I was usually watching TV shows like *Little House on the Prairie* or *The Waltons*. Even then, I was trying to arrange my world so that I would not be alone.

Rachael   The families on TV were company for you. What happened when the television was turned off? When you were alone?

Sonya   I think I was quiet, and often felt alone. But I created a world in my head that I lived out of. It was busy in there. And today I still have a lot going on in my head.

Rachael   How were your parents toward you during this time in your life?

Sonya   My parents were divorced, and I seldom saw my dad. My mom worked a lot in order to support us.

Diana   I want to go back to the front yard. Were you less lonely when you were outside? In what context were you the loneliest?

Sonya   I think being inside made me feel lonely, especially at night when I would go to bed. After my brother, Jason, came along, he would often sleep with me at night, so that helped.

Rachael   Did you feel anything else besides loneliness?

Sonya   Yes, anger. I always thought something was wrong with me because I wanted something more—something I didn't have. When I felt lonely, I would think, *Something's wrong with me*. I would often get angry, but I kept everything inside.

Diana   Who were you angry with? Yourself?

Sonya	Sometimes with myself, but I am sure I was angry with other people too. I was angry about a lot of things, but it came out toward other people, like my brother, Jason. I started playing football with Jason when he was about three and I was twelve. My loneliness made me feel powerless, but when Jason started playing football with me, I would feel powerful. And I remember a few times really hurting him. Remembering it brings me to tears because I love my brother. I would tackle him hard. I remember him crying and me saying, "You need to stop crying. You just need to learn to be tough."
Rachael	Because *you* were tough.
Sonya	Right. At least I was trying to be.
Diana	I can see why you were drawn to football instead of dolls as a little girl. Have you ever thought about why you were out playing football?
Sonya	I've thought about it, yeah. I don't know exactly why. What are you thinking?
Diana	I just hear and see a little girl who feels—and to a large degree really is—totally alone. There's no one there to take care of her. There's no one to be powerful for her. And so she says to herself on some level, *I'll be powerful for myself.* And what more powerful thing is there than this physical, tough sport. It's everything that will protect you from loneliness and anger. I hadn't thought about that until now. How do you feel when I say this?
Sonya	Oh, I still feel like something's wrong with me. When I remember that little girl, I just remember how dif-

ferent I felt. I always felt like I was supposed to be in the house playing with dolls, playing with Barbies, making cupcakes and wearing dresses.

Rachael   Did anyone ever do that for you—make cupcakes?

Sonya   Mom would make cookies sometimes. She wore dresses and she liked dolls, and I guess I thought I should too.

Diana   Was anybody *powerful* for you? Was anybody strong for you? Did anybody say, "Sonya, you don't have to be the football player? If you want to play football, go for it. I'll throw the ball for you, but you don't have to be strong." Did you feel, *I have to be strong*?

Sonya   Yes, I think I did feel that—that I had to be strong. I actually had this competitive thing with my mom, because she wanted me to be a baton twirler and a cheerleader. She made a deal with me: in order to play basketball at the YMCA I had to take baton lessons and march in the county parade. I think Mom always wanted a girl that liked the "girly" things, and she did not know what to do with me as a "tomboy."

Rachael   You were bucking her, plus you were giving yourself power over her.

Sonya   Doing it my way seems to give me the illusion that I am in control. But it hurts people along the way, and I just hate that! Even today that stubborn part of me shows up and I am resolved to do it my own way.

REFLECTING ON MY EXPERIENCE: SONYA

As my friends asked me about my childhood years, those memories flooded my senses: I saw the front yard of my house. I smelled the freshly cut grass that stained my white football pants. And I felt that deep sense of loneliness. I had never seen my aloneness as a safe haven before, but Diana's questions prompted me to realize that by playing alone and watching family shows on TV, I was able to create a fantasy world that brought rest to my young soul.

As Rachael probed more about my feelings during those years, a feeling of anger surfaced along with the memories. I felt angry that unlike most children I was not able to rest in the protection of someone older and stronger, but had to adopt a "tough girl" persona for protection. I was glad to have my companions with me as we dove more deeply into this "powerful" role I had assumed. As they asked me questions, I felt shame for this young girl—me—who tried to be tough even at the expense of her little brother.

After our conversation I wondered how different I am today from that little girl in the football uniform. I know God continues to change my heart, but even in the changing I can be self-seeking and look for ways to protect myself. I am just starting to understand that my aloneness can be a friend that invites me not to protection, power and toughness but to poverty, humility and gentleness.

Because I am more aware of how he has chosen me, named me and how he calls me his own (Isaiah 43:1), I am able to look back at that young girl and wish that someone powerful had protected her, and I am able to grieve for her. I believe Diana and Rachael's presence and support helped bring me to this place of rest. They reminded me I am loved and encouraged me to lean into the arms of my Savior as I grieved. Our good conversation and the connection we have as friends gave me hope that God's redemption will continue in my heart, and in all our hearts.

RESTING IN THE TENDERNESS OF OTHERS

Saturday evening at Embassy Suites, Dallas, Texas

Rachael   Sonya, you have been sharing with us about the stubborn part of you showing up, and you mentioned that your stubbornness affects people now. Can you unpack that for us? How does it show up in you now?

Sonya   It shows up between David and me. If David hurts me or disappoints me, it's almost like I've got to get a bigger stick to let him know that I'm tough, I'm in charge and I can handle it. It's a lot like I used to do with Jason. Obviously, I don't run up and tackle David, but I think he'd probably say that I have tackled him many times with my words.

Rachael   That's what we women do. We can take people down with our words.

Diana   Our words or our silence. We do find ways to be powerful when we want to be.

Rachael   But it's funny—as soon as you picked up on why Sonya took up football over dolls, I was thinking, "There's power in that." I wonder, Sonya, if you really wanted to be a girl? You saw your mom being the single mom and having to struggle all the time to keep the family going. I wonder if you ever thought, *I think I'd be better off being a boy.*

Sonya   You know, a good friend asked me that question one day. And I told him I don't think I wanted to be either one. I saw how men treated my mom, how they used and abused her, so I really did not like men. By nine years old there were some things—

some abuse from men—that had already happened to me that I think influenced my decision to not want to be a girl. But it also left me feeling cold toward men. I was so confused about how to be in my world, which probably explains my skepticism about Raymond when he showed up.

Rachael   I can't imagine why you didn't run inside the house. If a man on a Harley had shown up in my driveway, taken off his helmet and had slicked-back hair, I think I would have run inside and locked the door. You were so brave to stand there.

Sonya   Running in the house did not feel like an option. I'm sure I stood with my arms crossed, thinking, *What do you want, dude?* I wonder where my fear was. I am sure I was afraid inside but was working hard not to show it on the outside. I still get afraid sometimes, and I still don't let others see it.

Diana   I want to understand your heart at that moment when you talked to him, when he put his hand out and said, "I'm Raymond and . . ." Well, you didn't really talk to him, you listened to him. Is that correct?

Sonya   That's correct. I don't think I offered anything of myself then. And I think he realized that, so what he did was throw the ball with me. It was like he was trying to connect with me, and it was different than what I had experienced with other men. I'm sure I stood there with a cynical look on my face. I can't remember exactly, but I think that was my posture then of defending, protecting, being tough, giving the impression that, *Hey, you're not going to mess with* *me!* I go to tears again when I say that because I think sometimes that is what I do now to people, probably more so to men than women. As I've gotten older, I realize that's not the kind of woman I want to be, nor do I want to do that to my husband or my sons. I don't want my daughter to think that's what a woman is. And it saddens me to still see myself as that nine-year-old girl coming out in this forty-nine-year-old woman.

Rachael   I'm glad he told you he was a pastor. Did you know anything about pastors?

Sonya   I'd never had face-to-face contact with one, but I was familiar with what a pastor was. I'm sure he read my face and thought, *I'm not sure about you.* That's when I remember him literally taking the football or holding out his hand to get the football from me. He was there about fifteen minutes and just passed the ball back and forth with me. I began to think, *Now what's he going to want?* Again, I can't remember all the details, but I think that was the skeptical part of me that said, *Okay, he must want something from me.* I feel this way in other relationships where I assume people want something from me instead of really enjoying me.

Diana   Is it hard for you now not to assume that if a man offers you something, he's trying to get something from you?

Sonya   Yes it is. I don't trust well. I am always preparing my heart for being taken advantage of. A friend asked me once if I ever go off duty. This is still my struggle, but I feel like I am changing slowly. I do trust more, and I hope I am protecting myself less.

Rachael How does going off duty play out in your work as a counselor, where you are taking care of other people?

Sonya I'm so glad that God allows me to sit with people, listen to their stories and help them to find him. However, I sometimes get angry if David puts me in that role. I want him to take care of me, and I want him to offer me a place to go off duty.

Diana Give us an example where you think David puts you in the role of a counselor.

Sonya It happens when I feel he is leaving me to be the final word on finances or our children or other big decisions. When we got married (twenty-five years ago), I think I expected David to be everything for me. He has been there for me in many ways, but I am realizing neither David nor anyone else I'm in a relationship with will ever really "do it" for me. I went into our marriage trying to make David my prince who would always come and rescue me. I know that is a fairy tale, but my heart wanted a man to be strong for me. However, sometimes I have been unwilling to rest in what he is giving me for fear that I will be disappointed.

Rachael Do you trust David?

Sonya I don't do that so well. It is hard for me to rest with him if I am spending so much energy trying to prepare for disappointment or protect myself from it. Early on in our marriage I would be relentless with my questions toward him in order to be ready for anything. I didn't go off duty for fear he would take advantage of me instead of enjoy me, although, God is freeing me from that fear.

Rachael   What are some of those questions? I noticed in your story that you talk about how you've always been a questioner.

Sonya   I think sometimes my questions have been full of skepticism and anger. I think David feels that my questions are condescending.

Diana   The person who is asking the questions is really the one in charge, because that person can guide the conversation wherever he or she really wants it to go. I'm sure that sometimes your questions do sound condescending.

Sonya   What happens, Diana, is that I'm caught. I'm caught because I am curious and I want to know about people and their stories. I'm always watching people. Yet at the same time, it can be a sin. It can be a desire to keep control so I am prepared when I get hurt. Christ asks me to fearlessly give my life away, to lose it, and my questions can be a way to try to hold on to it.

Diana   And is that still true today?

Sonya   Yes, even today I sometimes hide behind questions. However, now in my late forties I'm more free as a woman to give myself than I've ever been, so I don't feel the same compulsiveness about asking questions, and I have more courage to enter into my own story instead. I think the change comes from knowing how imperfect I am—what a mess I really am—and how much the Father loves me anyway.

Diana   Do you ever have an hour when you don't ask any questions, where you just absorb without any filter?

Sonya   No, not much. I think it happens when I go to the beach. I literally sit, or I'll walk on the beach for hours and watch the waves and listen to them. I don't think, *I've got to make something happen*, or ask questions in my mind. Something in me stops, and for a little while all is at rest. And there are a few people in my life I feel like I can rest with.

Diana   Does that sound appealing to you, to think that you could sit and be with us and be off duty? We would love to be with you when you are not on duty, and I would enjoy you knowing what it's like to not have to ask questions.

Sonya   It sounds wonderfully appealing, and I really want to do that.

Rachael   Are there different motives behind your questions? I think there are legitimate and illegitimate motives. An illegitimate motive is to keep the focus off you—to ask so many questions that no one gets to know you. This gives off the façade of being in control while keeping a distance from other people. As women, aren't we supposed to be inviting? So a legitimate way to ask questions would be to invite another person into relationship, to ask with the agenda of love.

Sonya   I don't want to do it with a façade, Rach. I want my questions to invite relationship with others rather than hide my heart. But different parts of me feel two different things. I do just want to be restful with you, but another part of me thinks, *Oh, great . . . How do I make myself more restful?*

Diana   I think it's something that you already have within you to give. I don't think it's something you need to work on or anything like that. It's there, but something is getting in the way of you offering yourself.

Sonya   I think I feel that too. I can't put my finger on it. It's something about my heart that I am greedy with. It feels like holding cards so close to my chest that nobody can peek at them to see. I am afraid of how you might receive me in all my mess, so I keep everything close. There have been times when I am close to tears, but I keep them in instead of giving them. What I want is to openly be the mess that I know I am, and not try to clean it up. I don't want my offering to be contingent on how I think it will be received. I want to be open and offer myself just because I choose to love.

Rachael   Often people want the wisdom, the mind part, as opposed to the heart part. So many people want you for what you can do for them.

Diana   And they make it easy for you to stay hidden by not wanting something more.

Sonya   Oh, they do! Some people accommodate me well by asking very little of me. But I want to be fully present with you and I want to give more of myself no matter what the cost. I want to be a gracious woman who is desperately dependent on the Father.

Diana   Sometimes it's our fault. We let you stay hidden behind your good questions.

Sonya	Then I don't want you to do that with me.
Rachael	That reminds me of our emails leading up to this day. You wrote, "Now, be honest with me. I don't want to be a phony. I don't want to come across as—as our transcriber put it—'the moderator.'"
Sonya	That bothered me! The transcriber labeled me as the moderator. I battle with that part of myself that carries shame over asking questions. But part of me realizes my questioning is who God made me to be. I think I have helped a lot of people, but I have also hurt a lot of people. While very little is clear to me anymore, one thing that is becoming more clear is the knowledge that I want to be a woman who blesses people with her beauty. I really want you to know me. I want to love you both, and I don't want to keep myself from you. I do want to be honest. I want to be a woman who grows old and is more and more in love with Jesus, and whose life reflects that. A life that is soft, lovely and very inviting.
Rachael	History gave you a reference point at nine years old. You had a history that made you say, "Let's put this wall up."
Sonya	Yes, I did. It seemed to be part of how I chose to survive as a little girl, but now as a woman I don't want to relate to people with walls around my heart. It sounds like what you were saying, Diana, about me having something and not giving it to you. I am so afraid sometimes of letting myself be open and real.
Diana	But there has been such a change in your heart. I have

known you for eleven years and you are different. Just that you can sit down and talk like this . . .

Rachael   And to see your tears is huge for us. And it would be huge for David if they weren't angry tears, if they were tears like you're giving us now. I mean, you are genuinely sad over how you do harm to people. But it's not a selfish sadness; it's a sadness you want to share with us. I love when people share their genuine sadness with me.

Diana   Yeah, I do too. Are you surprised that we like to hear your sadness?

Sonya   No, I'm not surprised, but I think I'm scared. I don't trust you enough to know what you're going to do with me. On the other hand, your wanting my sadness lets me rest, and I sure like that.

Diana   So why do you think Raymond got to you?

Sonya   I don't think Raymond asked me to change my abrasiveness. He took me as I was. Raymond did not shame me for my cynicism. Actually, in some odd way, he invited it. I guess it was the strong love I felt from Raymond that eventually got to me. He sat with me Sunday after Sunday, explaining the gospel message and answering my many questions.

Rachael   Didn't your Sunday school teacher kick you out of class because she felt your questions were disruptive?

Sonya   Yes, she did. I think my feisty questions irritated her. For example, there was a picture of Jesus on the wall. He had the robe and the beard, and I said, "I don't know if Jesus looks like that. Do you think Jesus looks like that?" Well, the teacher pulled up her polyester skirt and adjusted her beehive hairdo before informing me that yes, Jesus looked *exactly* like that. (*laughter*) However, that stubborn part of me could not be quiet and it made me feel different from the other kids.

Rachael   And you couldn't relate to the guy in the white robe, but you could relate to the guy on the Harley.

Sonya   Absolutely.

Diana   You know what Sunday mornings are like for pastors— your husband was a pastor. You know they are very busy times, and usually preoccupied with the service. What does it mean to you now when you remember that Raymond sat with you week after week?

Sonya   Oh, it brings me to tears again, because I'll never forget sitting with him in this big old musty-smelling sanctuary. Nobody was there except Raymond and me. We sat on the second and third rows, and Raymond would listen to my questions. As time went on, I think something in me softened. I did not know what that cost him then, but now I see what he gave up in order to make me feel special.

Diana   I teared up as you were talking, and I noticed you did too. He really did make you feel like you mattered.

Sonya   Yes, he did. And the tenderness he showed me touched something in me. Even remembering it now makes me want to be soft, and invites me to enjoy being feminine.

Rachael   You weren't used to tenderness in men?

Sonya   No. He was so tender and gracious to me. I didn't know those words then, but I did know he liked me and enjoyed me. I didn't threaten him. I could be different than other little girls and that was okay.

Rachael   You felt safe, and he didn't threaten you.

Sonya   In the beginning he did, but later something in my small heart rested in his presence.

Diana   It sounds like he was a strong man. The Sunday school teacher sounds very weak: "I don't know what to do with this child! You've got to take her." But the pastor sounds like such a strong man. He may not have known what to do with you either, but he didn't pass you off to somebody else.

Rachael   Yes. And he allowed you to be you, different and all.

Sonya   Even today I can't remember the questions I asked him. However, our conversations helped bring me to know Jesus. I don't remember his answers either, but I do remember his smile and his tenderness. He gave me permission to be different, to be that little girl playing football and asking questions.

Diana   Raymond let the little girl playing football know that she was still a little girl by offering the tenderness he did. He would have treated a boy differently.

Rachael   And I think we women still want that tenderness from men. I know it's not what most women would say, but I think we are made for it. Recently my husband had a chat with our sons about what they can do for their girls to show a little bit more tenderness. "Don't be such a 'tough man,'" he said. The Raymond story would be good for them. Sonya, when I listen to you tell that story, I see how it draws you out to be a woman of softness. For the twenty-some years I've known you, I feel that you have been very much a woman of softness, but I see it come out so much more now.

Sonya   What you said, Rachael, just awakens something in me and moves my heart to tears again. I don't know why I'm crying.

Diana   Just being able to see your face and the tears is inviting. And it's not just tears, because there's something different about your face. It looks more restful.

Rachael   I just think it's wonderful. I think of how many times, even in each of our stories, a father is very significant. Raymond stepped into that role for you. There's something good men can do for little girls, and that man did something good for you.

Sonya   I think the thing I go back to is his strong tenderness. I can't get away from those words. I think Raymond's tenderness invited me to be that little girl. All I knew in that hour I had with him before church was that a man enjoyed me and that made me feel more unique than different.

REFLECTING ON MY EXPERIENCE: SONYA

Talking with my friends helped me to see how committed I have been to protecting my heart and yet how much I long to rest in the care of others. When Diana asked me if I would enjoy being off duty with them, I felt both relief and fear. Her question was an invitation for me to enjoy their love, and the idea of somebody wanting to love me feels like a cool drink of water on a 100-degree day. At the same time, I still struggle with the fear that if I allow others to see the real me, they might decide that they don't want me or that I am too much for them to handle. Rachael and Diana offered a place of rest to me, responding to my story with tenderness. I want to trust the Father enough to go off duty and receive their gift of rest, because trusting God with my heart brings Him great pleasure.

Throughout the conversation I found myself tearful, and tears are something I am often hesitant to give. As we talked, I felt less guarded with my tears; I wanted to be open and willing to receive my friends' love. It felt like I tasted a little more freedom as I showed them my tears and allowed them to hear some of my story.

Even though I often fail, I know that at the core I desire to love God and other people. I deeply want to receive tenderness from others and allow it to help me rest more intimately in the tenderness of the Lord.

Learning to Listen In

For Reflection or Small Group Discussion

Ingredient 1. Identify an Intentional Purpose

In many ways, Sonya's treasured football uniform was a disguise—a façade that hid the lonely, questioning girl inside. Sonya's friends wanted to understand that girl and the woman she had become.

- How can you encourage one another to look at their pasts with compassion and with a desire to live more fully in the present?

- How can you cooperate with the Holy Spirit during these kinds of discussions?

Ingredient 2. Tune In to Present Experience

Sonya's memories of Raymond, the pastor who reached out to her as a child, moved her to tears. Pause for a few moments and think about those events or people that seem to stir similar feelings in you.

- What are these feelings and where do they come from?

- How does your past, even the painful parts of your past, invite you into a closer relationship with others and with your heavenly Father? Be willing to linger on these feelings and what they mean rather than brushing them off or changing the subject.

Ingredient 3. Be Curious and Offer Feedback

Sonya told a story from when she was young, but with the help of Rachael and Diana she came to see how she is still living out that story in her everyday relationships. Sonya's friends noticed that many of Sonya's choices have been about protecting herself: the football uniform and tough exterior as a child, her stubbornness with loved ones, and even her tendency to ask questions. Sonya's friends invited her to look more deeply into her heart to see how she relates to people.

- How does Sonya respond to her friends pursuing her in this way?

- In your own life, how might you draw out the deeper part of a person's heart?

- Will you be open to your story in a way that invites a friend to be a deeper part of your life?

Ingredient 4. Explore Shaping Events

Early on in Sonya's life, she was told that she asked too many questions. This awareness that her questions bothered people brought shame to Sonya, which led her to feel different and to create an internal world where she kept others out.

- What about yourself did you become aware of early in life?

- What were the recurring questions in your life, and what did people communicate to you about them?

- How have these questions affected you as a woman?

Ingredient 5. Create a Vision

Sonya talked about sometimes hiding behind her questions, having a hard time trusting others and being reticent to go off duty for fear of not being wanted or enjoyed. Sonya's friends reassured her that they wanted her to rest in their presence. They didn't try to stop her tears but instead welcomed them and the truth they revealed. They even remarked that she seemed more restful after their discussion and encouraged her to keep giving her true self to others.

- How can you encourage a friend to live out of her authentic self and to feel restful in your presence?

- How can you give yourself permission to rest in this way?

Giving Away More of Me

Sonya's Response

LIVING OUT OF A NEW PLACE IN MY HEART

I "got by" as a child by setting myself apart as different: I was a tomboy, a kid who asked too many questions, a "fighter," and, in many ways, a girl without a father. I felt as though I was way too much for anybody to want or to handle, and in my fear I learned to hide behind a tough exterior that nobody could break through. I lived life defensively and was always prepared for the next disappointment, which put up walls between others and me. Even though I desperately wanted to feel close to others, my woundedness stopped me from opening up.

With the help of the Holy Spirit and my friends, I have come to see that this is not the way I want to live as an adult. It is prideful to label myself as "different" and to think I am a bother, because then I do not invite real relationships but instead require that others "come through for me" and make me feel worthy. Although I have made this demand of different people throughout my life, my husband, David, has experienced this selfish side of me the most. I have been married for almost twenty-five years and have often pressured David to make me feel like I matter, and I have become angry when he hasn't come through in the way that I wanted. Sometimes I feel like that lonely girl again, with the same ache in her heart. I understand now, though, that no person—not even my husband—has the ability to erase that ache, and I want to be willing to live with it rather than demanding that someone take it away.

My mom was still alive when Rachael, Diana, and I began this project. Mom and I were distant for many years, and I viewed our relationship as more of a duty than as an opportunity to offer her my love. For years I had been angry at Mom for not being the mother I wanted her to be, and I tried hard not to be like her. Recently she was diagnosed with cancer and passed away after only a few months. During her illness I spent many long nights with her at the hospital, and for the first time I was willing to really *see* her and to *listen* to her heart. God gave me the strength and the grace to let go of some of my anger toward her and instead to live out of my uniqueness. I realized that I no longer needed my mom to "get it right" or to be a certain kind of mom for me. I was free to love her as she was, to give to her and to enjoy her. I was free to celebrate her uniqueness as much as my own.

I remember one particular time when I was able to offer tenderness to Mom: it was about 5 a.m., and my mother lay sleeping in her hospital room. When she opened her eyes, I reached over and brushed back her hair, and, even though her eyes were tired, she smiled as I leaned down and kissed her forehead. Those few seconds felt holy to me because, in that moment, God helped me to surrender the anger that had guided my life for so many years.

God gave me the privilege of helping usher my mom from this world to the next as I sat by her side, held her hand and whispered in her ear that I loved her. God used my mom's death to reveal his goodness and to awaken a beauty that had been in me all along. At the same time, he gave me good friends to help me to a new place of freedom where I don't need to feel shame about my differences but can feel excited about being unique. I still have far to go, and I am grateful for help along the way.

FEELING DIFFERENT

Sunday morning at Embassy Suites, Dallas, Texas

Rachael   Before we began recording, we were talking about how all of us have had the word *different* applied to us, or at least we felt that way. Even if no one actually said, "Oh, you're so different," we felt it inside. You probably have experienced this the most, Sonya.

Sonya   Yes, and when I think about it, I don't think of it as a positive thing. For me it carries some kind of negative connotation that I'm different from other women. When I was outside playing football at age nine, I didn't have any other girls playing with me. When I grew up I stopped playing football and played basketball. I love the game. Later, when my daughter, Abbie, was born, I decided that I needed to play tennis or golf because I couldn't call my thirty-five- or forty-year-old friends and say, "Do you want to go shoot some hoops?" (*laughter*) So I've always felt different. I don't think I knew how to be a girl when I was younger.

Rachael   I remember that your mother made a deal with you because she wanted you to be more "girly."

Sonya   She did want that. Mom was girly, and I was her only daughter. She had this idea that her daughter should like dresses, dolls, Barbies, sequins, batons and cheerleading. I remember being on the cheerleading squad for one year. I was the only one who couldn't do a backflip. On several of the cheers the other cheerleaders would flip backwards, and I would have to flip forward. (*laughter*) My mom was in the stands just clapping away—she was so happy I was cheer-leading. I was the only one going forward, my hands straight in the air, and I was very aware that I could not do what the other girls were doing.

Rachael You have a daughter. What is she like?

Sonya She is unique. She's a good athlete, but she also enjoys being a girl who looks pretty. And I just love that about her. At first, I think I had a hard time with Abbie being a free spirit because I felt like she lived life in a way that I didn't know how to live it. That scared me. In fact, I found myself trying to make her more like me. I tried to rein her in because Abbie is very outgoing. I think my wanting to rein her in was more about making myself comfortable and not about loving Abbie.

Rachael She can be outspoken.

Sonya She can be very outspoken! There was a part of me that would always try to tame her a little bit. But I was sitting in my office one day and God said, "Sonya, I just want you to enjoy her. Enjoy her. She is my gift to you, and she's going to take you to places that you wouldn't go otherwise." Now, I just smile when I see Abbie and the ways God has made her unique. I so enjoy her.

Rachael   What do you think of, Diana, when you think of being different?

Diana   I think feeling different assumes there is a normal and that anything else is abnormal. And I do feel different in a lot of places. When I go to ministry conferences, these women are so experienced—women's ministry is their heart, it's their passion, it's their dream. I barely set foot in women's ministry till I was almost forty, so they have a lingo I don't have and I find myself feeling like *I don't fit in here*. And in the Christian world, there's also a certain definition of the "*really* Christian woman" and I've never felt like her. In fact, almost every woman I know doesn't feel like she's that woman. She feels different.

Sonya   I like what Diana said. Some people assume that there's a norm for what it means to be a woman, to be feminine. I know I had that assumption as a little girl; I didn't know how to put words to it, but I think I knew something was different about me. And even as I've grown up and have gotten older, I still sometimes think there is something wrong with me because I don't fit the norm.

Diana   I think part of the problem with the question of fitting in is how we regard what it means to be "quiet." If you think of quiet, not in terms of volume but in terms of your heart being still—like still waters—then when you were most quiet was when you were talking and being yourself. But somehow quiet and gentle became . . .

Rachael	"Don't speak."
Diana	"Don't speak," and I don't think that's what the apostle Peter is talking about when he speaks of "the hidden person of the heart" (1 Peter 3:4 NKJV).
Rachael	How many Christian women are invisible or feel they're invisible? I look at some Christian women and say, "Wow, they've been beaten down somehow; they're so mousey."
Sonya	We try to call that "submissive."
Rachael	I bet there are a lot of Christian women who hear that word and cringe.
Diana	A lot of them don't feel submissive, and so they feel different. And the norm for a submissive woman, I guess, is the woman who says yes to everything.
Rachael	Or "doormat." We used to call that kind of woman a doormat.
Diana	Yes, very compliant. Many people think that is what submission is, and it's not that submission is never compliant. In fact, sometimes submission *is* yielding.
Sonya	You're saying submission is about being willing to surrender something on behalf of another person. It is something I *choose* to do, not something I *have* to do. This is very different from being a mouse or a doormat.
Diana	I think it's about submitting willingly. In fact, being a mouse or a doormat could actually mean the woman is thinking, *I'm not going to give all of who I am. I'm going to keep some to myself so I don't make any waves or cause any problems.* I see that as much more self-focused as opposed to love, which focuses on the other person.

Sonya	It's also another way to protect yourself.
Rachael	Sure, it's walking on eggshells, knowing which land mine to avoid. You know what the triggers are. You know how to push that person's buttons, and you think, *If I can avoid those buttons, we're going to be fine.*
Diana	And that really isn't submission at all. It looks like submission, but it's really not.

It is getting close to lunchtime. Can we take a break? Let's think about the questions we all have. Why do we feel "different" so often and "unique" so rarely?

REFLECTING ON MY EXPERIENCE: SONYA

Most of my life I have felt different, and that feeling has often motivated me to try to prove myself. Seeing myself this way also gave me a reason to hide from others, which hindered me from embracing the unique life story the Father is writing for me. My small story is only one part of his larger story of redemption, and this book project has helped remind me of this greater, more eternal perspective.

Most women feel different at some time in their lives: Rachael did, Diana did, and I imagine that you have too. Somewhere along the way, the "different" label has been applied to us and made us feel ashamed of who we are, who God created us to be. Shame is a powerful force that can push us to strive to prove ourselves rather than to surrender to the One who made us and defines us.

It felt good to sit with two older friends who were willing to share their stories of feeling different. While our goal is not to fix or flatter one another, our shared journey gives each of us hope that God's good work continues in each of our lives.

CELEBRATING UNIQUENESS

Sunday afternoon at Embassy Suites, Dallas, Texas

Diana   To pick up where we left off, I don't think I ever see myself as unique.

Sonya   I don't either. Maybe feeling unique has to do with us coming to see ourselves as the Father sees us. One of the things that made me feel different was that there was a part of me that learned to be a fighter as a little kid. And there have been people in my life—good friends—who condemned that fighter in me without speaking to what it could be. But there were also other friends who said, "Oh, yeah, you fight us sometimes, and it's really hard." But with tears in their eyes they've looked at me and added, "That's the very thing I love about you: your willingness to get into the mess of people's lives and fight for them just like you have fought for my heart at times." When two of my friends told me this, for the first time I really understood I was more unique than different.

Rachael   Because not everyone's willing to fight for someone else's heart.

Sonya   The first time I heard that, I wept. I didn't just tear up. I wept because their seeing me and what I could be was an invitation for me to feel more than just shame about who I am. I learned how to be a fighter early on in life, and it became a way for me to survive. But then someone with tears and a big smile said it was a good thing. I knew I was loved and something in me was released. The fighter part of me doesn't always come out pretty, but it's part of who I am that is unique to me. My friends were right. Even though I stumble, I do love people with great passion, and I want to go in and fight for their hearts in good ways.

Diana And God's glory is in that. It makes me think about the ways God fights for the hearts of his people. And through the Old Testament, God makes way for the coming kingdom of Christ through kings and rulers and battles and wars. I guess that whole image of fighting is another thing we think of as so negative, but it's part of how God works and loves.

Sonya My friends helped me to see that this part of me doesn't have to be sinful. I don't want to be a hard, cold, fighting woman. I want to be a lovely, soft, inviting, unique woman who can fight for another person's heart in a good way. Something was redeemed in me in that moment when my friends affirmed my fighting for people's hearts. I thought, *That is a good part of me. That's something God's gifted me with and it's just who I am.* Everything in me wanted to use it in a way that glorified God.

Rachael I am thinking about your tears. In Scripture there are two kinds of weeping: the kind where you're wailing on your bed, and the kind where you're crying out from your heart. And there is a big difference. When you're wailing on your bed, it's all about you, but Sonya, I feel your tears come from a heart that does not want to hurt people but wants to bless them.

Diana I think maybe a lot of our feelings of "I'm different" have the mood of us wailing on our beds.

Rachael	Yeah, as opposed to looking at the uniqueness of who God made us to be.
Diana	Yeah, and offering that with tenderness, like you're talking about, Sonya. I know I can be quick to notice women who I think are different. I wonder what would change in my heart if I instead saw them as unique.
Sonya	Sometimes I think we need help to be able to see the unique part of ourselves because we cannot see it on our own. I can't be on the receiving end of me; I don't know what it's like to experience who I am. I can only know what it's like to experience other people.
Rachael	I hadn't really thought of "different" and "unique" as two sides of one coin before this weekend. And boy, we can be told so quickly that we're on the bad side of the coin. So many of the words we talk about have two sides to them.
Sonya	On the other hand, though, sometimes you meet people who wear the negative side of the coin like a badge. What if, for example, instead of feeling shame about being a fighter I was proud of it and used it to define myself? I think that's when our woundedness leads us to sin.
Rachael	Yeah, it's like having a clenched fist.
Sonya	Right, so we're back to the question, "How can we redeem the sinful aspect of being different?"
Rachael	By seeing ourselves and our individual personality traits as unique instead of different. To come to a place of enjoying who God has made us to be.
Sonya	Think of the women who let their woundedness—instead of God's redemption—define them. Some of

them wear a badge with a clenched fist that says, "I am different." Their woundedness becomes their strategy for living life to make sure everybody knows how different they are or how hurt they are.

Rachael It's amazing how we do that. I am a submissive wife, but I haven't always been gentle and quiet. Instead I have been just the opposite, a contentious and vexing woman, like an umpire who blows her whistle and tells people how to do things. And that's what I don't want to be, but I have been at times. I don't want to be on the negative, outspoken side of the coin, but I want to be on the positive, unique, "having a voice" side.

Sonya How would being unique look on you?

Rachael I think by accepting and living out the way God made me. I want to accept that I am outgoing; I don't want to squash the personality he gave me or my passion for people. I think for so much of my life people wanted to squash my outgoing nature because it was different. Everyone in my family was quiet except me. I am beginning to see, though, that I am uniquely Rachael.

Diana Sounds like you know you have something to give, and you don't want to keep it hidden.

Rachael That's right; I don't want to hide it under a bushel.

Sonya I almost feel like we're being greedy when we don't live out of our uniqueness.

Diana Well, there's definitely a generosity to seeing ourselves as unique and offering what we have. Living as a unique woman is saying we have something to

give, whereas being different seems more about
hiding something.

Sonya   Or about having something to prove. And uniqueness
is more about having the freedom *not* to hide and
not to need to prove anything.

Rachael   Yeah, because living uniquely is more about living
out of who we really are.

Diana   And who we are becoming. It's not just who we came
into the world as, but all the things God is doing in
our lives.

Sonya   Someone once said to me, "Your past is always a part of
who you are becoming." So even if we once lived out
of our differentness as women crying on our beds or
shaking our fists, we can now choose to live out our
uniqueness in a positive way that blesses people. I
wonder, do the two of you celebrate being unique
more now than before?

Diana   I think sometimes I do. John points out things about
me that are unique, and he does seem to enjoy them.
When we were dating, he said I was spunky. Now he
calls my spunkiness "a pain"! (*laughter*) While a lot
of guys might have been scared away by my spunkiness, he was drawn to it. When I think of cele-
brating my uniqueness, I also think of how tall I am.
When I was growing up, my height used to make me
feel very different in a horrible way. But now it's
great! I can reach anything I want, and I can put all
my kitchen stuff up high. Besides, clothes look good
on tall women no matter what the style, pretty
much—that's an advantage.

Sonya   How did you come to celebrate being tall?

Diana   I think growing older had a lot to do with it.

Rachael   It's amazing what that does to you. Girls, you still
          have twenty more years . . .

Sonya   What about you, Rachael? Do you celebrate your
          uniqueness?

Rachael   Oh, I think so. Because I've had enough kudos af-
          firming my uniqueness—comments that made me
          stand back and say, "Whoa! I didn't know I had that
          impact." I am often surprised when people want
          their friends and family to meet me because I matter
          so much to them. So I think I am celebrating my
          uniqueness. What about you, Sonya?

Sonya   I think I'm growing to enjoy my uniqueness. My
          feeling of being different is changing. Being dif-
          ferent used to feel shameful, and I know I have
          sometimes hurt people out of that shame. But now
          I am seeing how deeply I am loved by the Father,
          and that frees me to dance and sing!

Rachael   That concept is way out there! How many people
          really understand it?

Sonya   I don't know if I really understand it all—I feel I'm just
          starting to now. I've always felt internally messy be-
          cause I felt so different. So I worked hard to not be
          a mess, which kept me from grasping God's love,
          even though I was a mess! Now that I know more
          of his love, I'm becoming freer to be where I am and
          who I am.

Rachael   And that's uniquely you!

REFLECTING ON MY EXPERIENCE: SONYA

As I sat with Diana and Rachael that day, I felt a new restfulness in my soul and a new desire to accept myself as God's unique creation. All my life I have been afraid to believe I was designed in a unique way and have feared being seen by others. I feared that I would not be celebrated for my uniqueness but rather seen as too much to handle. Diana reminded me that seeing myself as unique and offering myself is an act of generosity, but hiding away because I am ashamed of my differences is an act of self-ishness. Rachael and Diana listened to me, saw me and celebrated who I am. Because they offered me this place to rest and to receive their love, it frees me to give to others from deep places in my soul.

When my friends spoke into my life that day, their words also helped me to discover that while the "fighter" part of my spirit could take me down a pathway to sin, it could also lead me down God's unique path to redemption. I realized that the redeemed version of my fighting spirit could help God do his work, not only in me but in others.

Rachael and Diana loved me well by talking about what it means to be a woman of God and what the Father desires from us. Rather than pressuring me to "fit the norm," they offered me the freedom to live a life that is both God-centered and uniquely my own (Psalm 139). When we celebrate our own uniqueness and the uniqueness of all women, we do not need to shamefully hide who we are or prove ourselves, nor will we need to compare ourselves with one another. We can simply feel the freedom to enjoy each other!

Learning to Listen In
For Reflection or Small Group Discussion

Ingredient 1. Identify an Intentional Purpose
Sonya and her friends wanted to explore the difference between "being different" and embracing their uniqueness in a way that brings glory and pleasure to the Father.

- How do you think God has made you unlike everyone else, and how can you help others to discover what makes them unique?

- What might be some dangers that could lead you to view or to use your differences in a sinful way?

- How can you use your uniqueness in a way that blesses others?

Ingredient 2. Tune In to Present Experience
In her conversation with Rachael and Diana, Sonya talked about some of the ways she had been wounded in the past, and how she wanted God's redemption rather than her own pain to define her.

- What pain are you struggling with right now, and what hurts are you afraid to share?

- How could you view your personal pain as part of God's larger story of redemption?

Ingredient 3. Be Curious and Offer Feedback

Since so many women react strongly to the word *submission*—
and not in a good way—Sonya, Rachael and Diana worked
together to explore what that word truly means. In their discussion they realized that a submissive woman has the power to
pour herself into others just as Christ poured himself out for his
followers. Submissive women willingly give of themselves, but
only in a way that will further God's purposes; women of Christ
are never compelled to fulfill other people's selfish agendas.

- What are the ways that our culture defines *submission* as a
  negative word?

- In what ways are you willing to give of who you are to further
  his kingdom?

Ingredient 4. Explore Shaping Events

When Sonya was a girl, she often felt confined by her mother's
definition of femininity. She loved football—not cheerleading—
and felt that her desire meant something was wrong with her.

- What kinds of assumptions have you made about what it means
  to be a woman, and where do those assumptions come from?

- Are your assumptions true and based on God's expectations
  of women, or are they based on someone else's expectations?

Ingredient 5. Create a Vision

In her conversation with Rachael and Diana, Sonya voiced a
desire to have God redeem her "fighting spirit" and to live out
her uniqueness in a way that blesses others.

- Think about the ways God made you unique and how those
  qualities might benefit others. Because of God's design and
  your own experiences, what are you uniquely equipped to do?

- If you truly accepted and celebrated the unique way God created you, how would you live your life differently?

- How might you let God redeem the sinful aspects of your differences so that you can live more freely and be more fully alive?

5

I Can Do Anything

Diana's Story

Diana standing in back.

(LITTLE) GIRL POWER

Like most little girls, I saw my daddy as big and strong. Seeing him lying in a hospital bed changed everything for me.

When I was eight and he was forty-one, my dad had a sudden massive heart attack. One night we were happily playing at the River Plantation Fourth of July picnic, and the next day my mom and dad were at a hospital in Houston, fifty miles away. The adults around me called it a myocardial infarction, but their children used words I understood. "Your dad had a heart attack," they said. That scared me to death.

The next two weeks, a blur of distant relatives came to visit and babysit, adding to my mother's anxiety. Hospitals did not allow children visitors back then, and so Mom drove us an hour each way just to stand in the hospital parking lot and wave up to the fifteenth-floor window, where Dad looked out from his bed. When he started to improve, and desperately wanted to see us kids, Mom and the nurse conspired to sneak us up the back stairs to his room.

I had not seen my dad for almost two weeks now, and that, plus the sneaking in part, had me very excited. But as we opened the door and peeked inside, I wondered if we had the right room. He sure didn't look or sound like my dad. He was so pale, and very, very thin. The voice Mom was always shushing in restaurants was now weak, almost a whisper.

Let me return to that moment. I have no idea what to do. Should I run up and hug him? I want to throw myself on the bed and wrap my arms around his neck. But I see machines hooked up to tubes, hooked up to his body. And I can see his weakness, so I hold back. With Mom's okay, I ease onto the side of his bed and gently hug him. He smiles really big—he's so glad to see us—but that's about all he can do.

I want to jump up and down and tell him everything I've been doing since he's been gone. But we have to be very quiet. Dad needs to stay very calm, and we might be found out. We are only allowed a few minutes, and I want to get back on that bed and stay all night. We go down to the parking lot and again wave up to the window. But this time, Dad is standing, waving back. He's getting better! And I just know it's because we came to visit.

Now I'm on a mission. I'm going to get my dad well. When he comes home from the hospital and can't be around quarreling kids, I eagerly take my little brother on a six-hour bus ride to stay with family friends in Dallas. At a rest stop, I start to get off the bus with all of the grownups to buy Cokes for Dane and me. He gets scared and cries, and I think, *What a baby.* I am responsible, independent and fearless.

When we return home and I am told I am leaving the next day with my sister for another week away, I am devastated. Dad is home, and I'm not. I want to be with him. I miss him, I miss my room, I miss my toys. Those thoughts don't last long. He needs me, and if I go away and give him peace and quiet, he will get well.

After I get home, he starts walking for rehab. I walk with him the mile around our neighborhood. He talks to me about politics and sports, and it's hard to keep up with both the strides and the conversation. It's the highlight of my every day.

He's still recuperating, and it's too hot in the Texas summer for him to mow our thick St. Augustine lawn, so I beg to do it. I'm a skinny, bird-legged girl and the mower is powerful and unwieldy. I am beyond exhaustion three hours later when I finish. I beg to do it again the next week.

I notice that things are happening in my home. Dad is getting healthier. Mom is getting calmer. And I just know it's all because of me.

THE PRESSURE OF POWER

Saturday morning at the mountain condo

Rachael　What I noticed so strongly is this is *so* much about your dad. And it seems like you have something going with him. Tell us about that.

Diana　Well, my dad died when I was eighteen, but growing up, we always had a special relationship; I spent a lot of time with my dad. Every Saturday morning he would play golf. He'd get home around noon, and then he'd usually sit in front of the TV and watch sports all afternoon. I was right there with him, every Saturday afternoon. I don't remember anyone else sitting and watching TV with him. I remember that being a normal part of my Saturday.

Rachael What put your father and you together in such a way? Were you striving to have a relationship? Was it something *you* made happen?

Diana I think I did. I mean, I definitely remember wanting it badly.

Sonya Did he seek you out when he'd come home from golfing?

Diana No, I don't think so. He would end up in the living room, watching . . .

Sonya Sports . . . and you would end up there with him.

Diana Right.

Rachael So it probably was initiation on your part.

Diana Yeah, I think so.

Sonya Did you feel pretty? Did your dad make you feel pretty?

Diana Um . . . not when I was young. I don't remember much of that. No.

Sonya Did he do it when you were older? During adolescence?

Diana I wouldn't use the word *pretty*. I think he recognized my attractiveness to men. I remember one time when we went to a store, and he said, "Did you see that

	guy? He really noticed you!" or something like that.
Sonya	What did that feel like to have him tell you that? The way he told you?
Diana	I think I felt a little embarrassed.
Sonya	As I noticed your face, I was wondering if that was a hard question for you?
Diana	It feels like there is a big vacuum there. Just kind of empty. It wasn't like I felt ugly.
Sonya	I wasn't thinking that.
Diana	It was more just kind of nothingness there.
Rachael	So, you were a "buddy."
Diana	Oh, yeah, very much, and the sports thing was the way to get in with him, because he just loved sports so much. So I just knew that that was an easy connection.
Sonya	It sounds like you spent a lot of time with him.
Diana	I do remember making an effort. It wasn't just an accident, but it was an effort to be something for him ... to be knowledgeable about football, to be interested, to be a very eager football-watching companion. It was work. I remember working at it. The payoff was *great*!
Sonya	What was the payoff?
Diana	Payoff was I got time with my dad. He was pleased with me. He was impressed with me. He would brag on me to his friends about how I knew all the plays, all the hand signals for the penalties. I'm *sure* I knew much more about football than the average ...
Rachael	Eight-year-old little girl. I mean, who wants to learn that at eight, except someone who wants to be close to someone?

Sonya   Let me ask you this: how do you think that has affected you today? I'm trying to picture you as an eight-year-old bird-legged girl so desiring to have your dad's eyes light up over "that's my girl!" So you're doing all kinds of things to try to get him to see you. How does that play out now with you and John?

Diana   Well, I definitely don't do that with John. Maybe, if anything, I do the opposite. I probably say to him with my actions and who I am, "I'm not showing you anything."

Sonya   You know, I think you do both. I think you *do* do it with John. Sometimes I see you say, "I'm not giving you anything" and you shut down. But there's a part of you that works really hard to please John. To step around John. To make sure he's okay. And I was making that connection as you were talking about your dad. It's not exactly alike, but I do see you do it with John.

Rachael   Do you do this with other people, Diana? Like Sonya or me? What do you think, Sonya?

Sonya   Diana, I think with me I feel that you're more *careful*. When you were talking about you and your dad, I thought, *That's what I see her do with John sometimes.* It may not be sports, but it's sitting beside him on a couch watching a movie he wants to watch or making sure he's okay with his agenda. It seems like you feel pressure to make sure he is okay.

Rachael   I don't feel any shutdown from you. I think we've had some good talks. You are a person who is capable and very organized in the head, but I can see how you could shut down your heart. You have to see your little world as organized. Your dad comes home from the hospital. The one thing you're thinking is how you're distressed because you aren't there to make him better! And you want to make things *better*! You want to fix people. You want to fix situations. But I don't feel you've tried to fix me.

Sonya Do you ever do that with some people at work?

Diana Sometimes I do, yeah. Sometimes I feel pressure to make sure things keep running smoothly. I feel like a lot of people look to me for that.

Sonya Tell me what you feel about what I said and some of what Rachel has been saying.

Diana I think you're right. I do this managing with John. I second-guess his decisions, because I know that I know better, and I've researched this. And you can't make this decision because there might be a better one, and I can probably come up with it. Give me three minutes on the Internet and I'll find it. I do that to him a lot. Recently we spent an entire day together shopping for a car. And I knew I was going to try to tell him what to do this whole day. So I mentally said, *I'm going to bite my tongue.* I was biting my tongue *all day long*! I felt like every single second I was ready to say, "Well, you know, you might want to think about this," or "You know, this would be better because, why don't you tell the man this?" or "Say it this way."

REFLECTING ON MY EXPERIENCE: DIANA

Rachael's very first question stirred some pretty strong feelings
for me. Rachael noticed that the story was all about me and my
dad, and when she asked a question about that, I felt both delighted to be seen and terrified to be known. Rachael and Sonya
didn't push me into territory I wasn't ready to enter but simply
asked factual questions about what was happening in my home
and life with my family. They were paving a way to the decisions my young heart had made at that time, without pushing
down a door I wasn't ready to open.

Sometimes when we talk with one another, we'll see things
very clearly about someone that she doesn't see herself. It is very
tempting in those times to reveal what she's missing, but that is
often a mistake. As my friends continued to ask simple questions, my resistance to revealing my true heart weakened, and I
could more clearly see and share the longings, the hurts and the
sin in my heart. When Sonya and Rachael expressed their curiosity and interest in me both as a young girl and now, I felt their
tender care for me. That opened me to hearing what they saw as
evidence of the presence of Christ and the work of the Spirit in
me for growth and change.

There are other times when speaking what you see in the
present creates a vision for what could be. When Sonya challenged my answer about how all of this affects the way I interact
in my marriage, she bravely and gently chose a time to show me
something I couldn't see for myself. Because we can never fully
understand our hearts (Jeremiah 17:9), I needed a clarifying
comment in a purposeful conversation with people who knew
me well to provide a glimpse of what I couldn't see myself. That
helped me think about what could be different, and how God
might be working to change me.

THE STRENGTH OF SURRENDER

That afternoon in the mountains

Sonya So before we took a break, Diana, you were telling us about how you often feel like it's up to you to make things better, and how sometimes that leads you down a path of hurting John. Is there a connection between how you were with your dad and how you treat John now?

Diana Well, I was thinking back to this story about my dad in the hospital when I was trying to fix everything.

Rachael Uh-huh, you're a fixer.

Diana I felt like I could . . . if I was just strong enough, good enough, independent enough, competent enough, then my dad would *live*, and then I could have some kind of relationship with him again.

Sonya It's there in the last sentence of your story, "Dad is getting healthier. Mom is getting calmer. And I just know it's all because of me."

Diana I was the center of the universe.

Sonya Are you saying it was the competence that makes the connection between your dad and John? It sounds like there's a part of you that felt that you needed to be the competent one, to make sure he was going to get better. And you were going to take over every-thing. So when I hear you talk about buying a car with John, for instance, there's an element of "I've got to take care of this."

Diana Yes, and I hate what that does to John.

Sonya What do you hate about it?

Diana   I think it makes him feel like he's not smart, and less of a man.

Sonya   Why do you hate that?

Diana   I think I could be so much more to him. If I relaxed and quit fixing, that would be such a delight to him. I think he would take charge so much more, and he's even told me this, if he knew that every decision he made wasn't going to get second-guessed. The day we bought the car, when we started out he said, "Diana, I want to make it clear that I do not want to start out this day thinking that no mistakes can be made."

Sonya   Those were good words from John.

Diana   They were *great* words. But I find it so hard to live that way. And that's also how I see our marriage—that it's all up to me. If I don't do this or that, then everything's going to fall apart.

Sonya   Which is exactly what you felt with Dad.

Diana   It is.

Sonya   And it's also what you feel at work sometimes.

Diana   Oh yeah . . . yeah.

Rachael So no one's relaxing, resting . . . no one.

Sonya   Do you know what's behind the need to be responsible and competent?

Diana   I guess it makes me feel in control.

Sonya   And you need to be in control because . . .

Diana   I need to be in control, because everything's going to fall apart otherwise.

Sonya   That's where that little girl still shows up. I think you need to be in control, because you're *so afraid* that there's not going to be a connection between you and that man. There's not going to be a place that you're delighted in and wanted.

Rachael   A place where you feel pretty.

Sonya   Yes, feel pretty, 'cause underneath all the work to be competent, I see fear.

Diana   Oh, I do feel *huge* fear.

Sonya   You seem to feel like, *Okay, I've got to work harder so that I can maintain this relationship. I've got to work hard here and perform so they won't see the weakness, the anxiety, so that they're going to connect, they're going to be with me.* And I wonder what you'd be left with. I know God's redeeming this in you, because I've seen it happen through the years. But I wonder what you'd be left with if you weren't doing that?

Rachael   What would it be? What would you be left with?

Diana   I think, on some level, I'd be left with nothing.

Rachael   Hmm.

Sonya   Is that the fear?

Diana   I don't know. Sometimes letting someone else fail me feels like something that I can't let happen. I can't let that be a possibility. I can't be failed. As long as I'm confident and independent, then I really don't want that much from people, and they can't fail me. But John says that I tell him he fails me all the time (*laughter*), so I don't know if that's true.

Sonya   There's more than fear, though. I think deep down your heart says, "Oh, I *so* much want that . . ."

Diana   Oh, I do! I do.

(pause)

Sonya   Where are you now?

Diana   I'm at that dinner that John and I had with Larry right after SSD [School of Spiritual Direction]. John was really affected by some things Larry said to him, some complimentary things, and he seemed hopeful about moving toward me in our marriage. Then Tim Burke came over and shared some about his marriage. He said that John seemed ready to move toward me. And then he looked at me and said, "And Diana, you are just glowing!" And I was! I've never been more hopeful than I was that night.

Rachael   It's still tender with you.

Diana   I remember that so clearly. I still want it just as much as I did that night. I just don't live like that a lot. And when John *will* do something that's moving toward me, it means the world to me. But it just seems so rare. It's almost like pouring a drop of water into a person dying of thirst. It's great but maybe it's never enough. I don't know. Maybe there's a thirst that John can't fill that I expect him to. But there's also a thirst that he can contribute to that, I really . . .

Sonya   That sometimes he does and sometimes he doesn't?

Rachael   We're all human.

Sonya   I think you're letting awaken in you what's always been there—those longings of wanting to feel pretty in the presence of your husband, of wanting him to contribute to the thirst, of wanting his eyes to dance when you enter a room, look across there and go, *That's my* *woman over there!* As a little girl arranging everything, I don't know how much of that you let yourself want. And I just *love* seeing that awaken in you. It's cost you dearly. I think it's caused you to ache deeper, and the pain has been greater at times. Is that right?

Diana   Oh, yes.

Rachael   So that's brought out femininity in your competency. In some ways you're still very competent, but you have that feminine part that just hasn't gone away— the inviting, tender part.

Sonya   That's a great point, because you're a great thinker, a hard worker. You *are* very competent, and that's not all negative at all. But the last couple years it feels like competence is beginning to look different. It's less out of selfishness—protecting and preparing, managing and controlling. I think competency can be so lovely on you, and I've seen that. I think now it's more out of giving, surrendering and inviting.

Rachael   She's taking more risks.

Sonya   Which I think is what's cost her so much at times.

Diana   I think God has really grown my desire to give more than just my competence. It's very safe to just offer that.

Rachael   With competence, you don't need the heart.

Diana   No, you really don't.

Rachael   We've been working together just a little over a year. This idea's been germinating in you. Oh, I see *huge* change.

Diana   Really? I hope I'm changing in ways that I could not on my own. That's when I. . . I want to bow in worship, because I see God changing that. I see myself being a little less the center of the universe. I'm so glad for that.

Rachael So, when you came to know Christ in your teenage years, you played "competent" with him too, didn't you?

Diana I did, but only after I got into Christian circles. (*laughter*) When I heard the gospel, it was the first taste of freedom I ever had from competence.

Rachael Really?

Diana Yes, because the Bible said, "You can be connected with God forever, and it is because of Christ—who he is and what he's done—and not your competence." I could not believe it. I could not *wait* to hear more! All I wanted to do was read the Bible. All I wanted to do was know Jesus, because he was offering me a hope other than myself! I discovered that Jesus was my real *hope*!

Rachael Hmm. Wow. How many people can say that?

Diana I've never thought of my salvation story as too exciting, because I wasn't a drug addict. But I was a competence addict. And I still function that way sometimes. The difference the gospel makes is that now I don't have to keep living that way. I don't have to manage and arrange so that I'll get what I want. I'm free to love when I get what I want or not, because that's not the point anymore. The point is Christ and his kingdom, his purposes. The gospel is taking on a new life for me!

Rachael Yeah. We can *see* it. (*laughter*) If our readers could see this, they could see that you're really excited. So you didn't play "competent" with him.

Sonya	I loved when you were talking earlier about bowing. That didn't feel "competent" at all.
Rachael	No! That was surrender. That was a beautiful picture.
Sonya	And I think when competence comes out of a heart of surrender and giving and invitation, it's just beautiful.
Diana	And it is restful, very restful.

REFLECTING ON MY EXPERIENCE: DIANA

This entire conversation challenged my commitment to competence, because when friends like Sonya and Rachael ask to see your heart, they don't want a right or wrong answer. They're not looking for something to impress them. They want what is real. With their questions about what I was thinking and feeling at the moment, Sonya and Rachael lovingly asked me to give them more than my abilities or insights, and to consider how together we might make connections between the decisions of my heart as a young girl—what worked to get me what I thought I wanted and needed, and how those strategies sometimes affect the way I relate now, especially with my husband.

Sonya and Rachael let me ramble and think out loud during this conversation. When there was silence, they allowed it, and then rather than fill it, Sonya asked me a simple question, "Where are you now?" This was a wonderful gift to me, because I can sometimes leave a conversation emotionally when it feels vulnerable. Good conversations invite friends into risky places and then lock arms with them to face together whatever awaits them. When Rachael told me about the changes she had seen in me, I was surprised at first, and even a little embarrassed—competent women don't think they really need to change *that* much. Then I realized that what I had been afraid of in the beginning—being seen—was actually, in the company of a loving friend, even when revealing sin in my heart, especially when revealing sin in my heart, and being met with great mercy and grace, pointing me toward growing faith and the hope that I could relate to others in ways that offer the love of Jesus Christ.

It might have been that experience of being seen and loved that took our conversation into even deeper transformation territory. In looking together at how I relate to John and others, we saw the connections between sin and grace, and the dichotomy between putting "confidence in the flesh" (Philippians 3) and living competently but dependently on Christ in the power of the Spirit. The conversation could have gone a few directions at this point. They could have felt sorry for me, the poor little girl who worked so hard for relationship. Or they could have preached to me, the little girl who needed straightening out. Instead, they joined me, and together as women we approached God and his Word, increasingly aware of his holiness. And so the conversation naturally went to the hope of the gospel, and of living and loving like Christ.

Learning to Listen In

For Reflection or Small Group Discussion

Ingredient 1. Identify an Intentional Purpose

Diana's story described her experience of her father's near-fatal heart attack and the ways she responded to that life-shaping event. When the three women came together to discuss this story, they explored and saw the purpose and payoff of such a strong resolve to be competent above anything else, and how Diana might pursue a different purpose for her competence.

- What do you have an incredibly strong resolve to do or be?

- Discuss with your group the possibilities for how your conversation could help you move from a self-focused resolve to a God-focused resolve that would bring glory to God.

Ingredient 2. Tune In to Present Experience

Rachael and Sonya asked Diana many simple questions to help her see how the decisions she made as a young girl affect what she is feeling and doing now as a woman. Diana realized that she spent much time and effort trying to arrange things so that her dad would notice her, and that she often does the same thing with people in her life today.

- What do you do in order to make sure you are noticed or loved?
- Where has that desire become a demand? Hint—where are you most frustrated right now?
- What would help you to more freely receive the gift of the lavish love of Jesus Christ?

Ingredient 3. Be Curious and Offer Feedback

Rachael responded to several statements in the conversation with a request for more—"tell us more about that." Because of her friends' pursuit of something more, Diana felt free to ramble and was less guarded with her words, leading her to see more clearly where her competence was serving a fearful and selfish purpose.

- How can you express loving curiosity in a conversation?

Ingredient 4. Explore Shaping Events

Diana experienced great fear during her father's illness and acknowledged the way "huge" fear sometimes affects how she relates to people today.

- Where do you struggle with fear?
- When do you remember being most afraid, and what did you do to feel less afraid?
- How do you see that pattern repeating itself in your relationships now?

Ingredient 5. Create a Vision

Rachael and Sonya helped Diana see that the gospel invited her to use her competency not as a way to control her fear or being loved, but as an expression of how she is loved in Christ—a part of the inviting woman God created her to be as she reflects his image, glory and love.

- Where do you see yourself trying to control?
- How could the gospel of Jesus Christ affect your need to control?
- How would giving up control change your close relationships?
- Discuss these possibilities with others and allow them to grow your vision for how you can love more freely.

6

Invitingly Competent

Diana's Response

HOPE FOR AN ADDICT

Before our conversation that day, I don't think I would have called myself an addict of any kind. Addicts are people who lose jobs, ruin relationships and can't seem to get it together.

But Gerhard Forde, in his book *On Being a Theologian of the Cross*, helps me understand my reality. Forde explains Luther's distinction between being a "theologian of glory" and a "theologian of the cross," and he speaks of addiction this way:

> What is interesting here is that Luther likens the plight of the theologian of glory to that of an obsessive lover or a miser. In our day the drug addict or alcoholic would be the closest parallel. The desire, the thirst for glory or wisdom or power or money, is never satisfied by the acquisition of what is desired. The more we get, the more we want. There is never real satisfaction, never the confidence that we have or have done enough.

I recognize myself in that picture of an addict: always more. Never enough. Never satisfied. Never have enough challenge or knowledge or affirmation or love. Never have done enough to get these things or even enough to avoid failure or loss. That's how I've lived, and sometimes still do.

Seeing myself as an addict to competency reveals that I easily live in a "theology of glory," where I judge the world (and myself) by appearances. I slavishly need to look good, smart and spiritual, and by doing this, I don't have to see what God sees. I don't need the cross. (I literally stopped for a moment when I wrote that. It is an awful statement that brings me right now to tears. So often I have lived *as if I don't need the cross*.)

But I can smile and rejoice with a new heart, because though I have been a competence addict, and sometimes act like one, I have also seen clearly that I need the cross! I don't have to look past the cross. I can see the reality of the suffering and pain of Christ, and whatever of his sufferings I am privileged to share. I don't need my own glory; I can move deeper into the rest and glory of Christ!

Not having to avoid pain with competence lets me be a different kind of competent woman. I am starting to use the abilities God has given me in ways that give honor and glory to Christ, that draw people in, not push them around or away. As the Spirit changes me, I am becoming more inviting, and hopefully a truer reflection of the invitational good news of Jesus Christ.

I'm still competent, and I'm grateful to God for that. But I'm even more grateful for how he is helping me become a gospel-drenched woman who uses her competence not for her own glory or power or numbness or avoidance of pain, but for the purposes of God, in the power of the Spirit, for the glory of Christ.

THE FACES OF COMPETENCE

Sunday morning in Rachael's dining room

Sonya   What do you think of when you hear the word *competence*?

Rachael   I think of *competence* mostly as a good word.

Diana   I'm a little more neutral on that word, because it doesn't sound inviting. If somebody said, "Diana, I want you to meet so-and-so. She is so competent," I wouldn't think, *Oh, I can't wait to spend time with her.*

Sonya   I think of competence as smug. I do think of it as a negative thing.

Rachael   Wow. Tell us about that.

Sonya   I spend a lot of my time trying to be competent, and I am a pretty competent woman, but if I got to pick what somebody would say about me, "competent" would not be on the top of my list. The top would be "She's kind." I would love to hear that. And "She really loves people well, she's loyal, she's responsible, you can count on her."

Rachael   I'd even rather hear "sweet" than "competent."

Sonya   And you admire people that are competent.

Rachael   Oh, very much, and I do look at people and say, "Wow. She knows where she's going. She knows what she's doing. She has it all together." A competent person has it all together!

Sonya   That's what they work hard to project.

Rachael   You don't see competent people ever break down.

Sonya   They're always helping the people who are breaking down.

Rachael   Yes. They're on the sidelines. No, they aren't on the sidelines; they're in the game!

(*laughter*)

Diana   They're leading the game!

Rachael   That's right. They may be the coach. And you need those kinds of people.

Diana   Yeah, and in a lot of places, like work, I want people to be able to have confidence in my competence. But I wouldn't want them to *just* say that about me. I would want them to see more of me than competence—I'd like them to see the human part. And I think that's the part about competent that I hide out in. The more competent I can be, the less human I seem to be.

Rachael   You always were a competent child, and a competent child misses a childhood, because they are always years ahead of themselves. And you were eight, running the family . . .

Diana   Thinkin' I was.

Rachael   That's not an eight-year-old. 'Cause you look at your daughter when she was eight and say, "Aaww!" But competence is something that was in you from way back.

Diana   Yeah, I definitely felt like it would get me a lot. And now I don't always like what it gets me.

REFLECTING ON MY EXPERIENCE: DIANA

We each had different opinions about whether *competence* was a positive or negative word, and we were all right, in a way. Competent women make great contributions to their families, friends, churches and the world. Throughout the Bible, there are many records of competent women using their abilities for the growing of God's kingdom. It's a good thing.

Rachael mentioned that when I look at my daughter as an

eight-year-old, I don't think about competence. I had never thought of that before. I'm not even sure I ever really thought I *was* an eight-year-old girl! That comment helped me see that my connection with competency was more about my own survival and comfort than contributing something good to others. My friends helped me see in new ways my commitment to competency for my own sake, and I started to question it.

Recently, I had a shift in responsibilities at work. The increased variety and challenge that I genuinely enjoy gave way to increasing pressure and anxiety. In my pride, I was convinced I was failing; I was working like crazy out of fear of losing an image of high performance instead of serving the church out of the riches and strength of the Lord Jesus Christ and gratitude for his grace and mercy. God is using the conversations I had with Rachael and Sonya to point me to the real life and rest that Christ alone offers, and offering what competence I have out of that. I am more and more desperately dependent on the strength of Christ to enjoy and invite others into the grace and love of the Father. And the funny thing is, in that freedom I actually see my competence in some areas is growing! But the energy behind it is different, and the effect on those around me very different.

THE INVITATION OF GRACE

After lunch at Rachael's home

Rachael   It has something to do with relationships, doesn't it? Competent relationships are not seen as kind, tender. If they view you as competent, that's all for your head and what you can do for them. If you're considered kind, it may be what you can do for them, but it's with a different energy.

Diana   Yeah, my competence serves to get me relationships where I am always in control. I'm in charge. And I'm very stubborn about giving that up, but I am seeing how awful it is. John and I meet with two other couples once a month to eat great food and talk about our marriages. And the last time we met, I confessed that I had basically lied to them the previous time we had been together. They had asked me how I felt about something, and I thought it would impress them if I said, "Fine, good," when inside I wasn't doing well at all. I had used my competence to hide what was really going on inside me, hoping they would think I was so great, so mature, so spiritual. And when I confessed this to them, they brought up the word *competence*. They said, "You're always holding on to this competence."

Sonya   What did they mean by that?

Diana   They basically said, "We don't need you to be competent all the time, and we don't want you to be competent all the time." And one of the men said, "I love seeing this part of you. I'm so drawn to this." I don't know, but there's something about laying down that competence that draws people in. The competence can keep people away.

Rachael   Ah, when you lay down the competence, you draw people in. You're invitational.

Diana   I don't think I was any less competent, but that time I offered myself in a different way. I didn't hide behind the competence. I think that was the difference.

Sonya   So what are we saying competence is? Being capable?

Diana	In this context, it seems like it's more than that.
Sonya	Right.
Diana	It's being capable at the expense of being . . .
Rachael	Gentle? Kind? . . . No?
Diana	Maybe.
Rachael	Capable at the expense of being invitational.
Sonya	Could we be competent and still be a mess in a lot of ways? Would that be more invitational?
Diana	Oh, I hope so. I relax just thinking about that! And it gives me hope that I could offer something good out of my competency. It's still there, but it's not the only thing there. It's so safe when that's the only thing we offer.
Rachael	Because you do get kudos on being so bright, so discerning.
Diana	I feel a lot of pressure to be competent in my job. And I feel the disappointment of people who see flaws in my competence. I disappointed someone recently and without saying these exact words, what I heard from her was, "Diana, that's not what we expect of you. We expect you to have all your ducks in a row." Those women put the same pressure on themselves.
Sonya	I wonder if you're not more inviting when you have flaws.
Rachael	Oh, I would think so.
Diana	Well, absolutely, because I think this woman is making herself nuts trying to hold up a level of her own competence. For me to be able to say to her, "I didn't get it done," and ask for graciousness from her . . .

Rachael Wow, that's good.

Diana That takes the focus off of me and my need to impress, to perform. It's not about me anymore. I can offer something better to her and maybe even offering her a picture of what it would be like to not be so tied to competence.

Rachael I've used competence to try to impress too. I remember my first year of teaching in Champagne, Illinois. I thought, *I'm really going to impress this principal with my lesson plans.* So, I took home every book for every subject, every Friday night, so I would have the best lesson plans. And then one Friday, she saw me as I was leaving and she said, "Rachael, maybe one day you'll be organized enough to not have to take those home."

(*laughter*)

Sonya So, why do you think we as women arrange our lives in such a way that we have to be competent? What purpose does it serve for us?

Rachael I know for me, it is the kudos.

Sonya Okay, what is it for you?

Diana The kudos, and also it's toughness for me.

Rachael So, that's putting up a wall.

Diana Yeah, nothing gets to me when I'm so focused on my competence, good or bad. I can control, because I'm really pretty competent. I have some abilities, enough to be able to get a lot of things done. So, I can hide there.

Sonya And when you do that, it's impossible to enjoy real relationship. You don't feel close to somebody that's competent. You might admire them, and they may get things done. I think, for me, I thought if I was competent, I would be wanted.

Rachael   Not for you, but for what you could do.

Sonya   I thought people would want me if I was competent.

Diana   And they probably did to some degree.

Sonya   Oh, all the time.

Rachael   For you, being competent would mean that you mattered.

Sonya   Yeah. I needed to matter. I remember when I was a new counselor, I went in to my boss—and he had a staff of counselors—and as the new twenty-something counselor, I thought I would show him all the great things I'd done in my first counseling session, thinking he'd be so impressed with me. He very kindly told me it wasn't as great as I thought.

Rachael, what purpose would competence serve for you?

Rachael   For me, it would be to have a voice, even if the voice were on my lesson plans. It would be a response like, "Wow, is she together, is she competent! We are glad to have her." And I would have a voice, I thought.

Diana   That people would listen to.

Rachael   That people would listen to. And for you, competence would be, as you said . . .

Sonya   A place to hide.

Diana   Yeah. And that's why I was so shocked at what happened with my friends when I put my competence down. All I had to do was open the door just a crack, and they were pushing their way in! They were saying things to me like, "We forgive you," and "We love seeing this part of you," and all those things that when I'm hiding in my competence, I don't even hope for. It touched a new part of me.

Rachael   The depth of you, the inside, as opposed to the part you can accomplish on the outside.

Diana   Yes, the deepest parts—the sin, and Christ's presence freeing me to love and be loved.

Sonya   That makes me think about the gospel. What connection does competency have with the gospel?

Diana   Oh, the gospel . . . that's what the gospel is! It's . . . it's . . .

Rachael   An invitation to come . . .

Diana   To quit living in your own competence. You can't enjoy right relationship with a perfect God based on what you can do. You don't need to work harder; you need grace.

Rachael   There's something about grace. A competent person doesn't offer a lot of grace.

Diana   It's a life void of grace, basically. I don't need grace, I don't get grace, and I won't give grace.

Sonya   What kind of harm does that kind of life do to people? What's that do to my relationships?

Rachael   I know that when I'm around a competent person, I shut down and don't give who I am or what I can do for a person. They become the boss, the micromanager, and they don't need my part of the body to accomplish what they're doing.

Sonya	They're real big too.
Rachael	Yeah, they're real big, and I can sit back, be small and just sort of bask in the joy of being on the team and float along. But then, I'm not doing what God has called me to do. Sit back and do nothing in the kingdom? Just be on the team? That's not what God calls me to do.
Diana	You probably don't want to offer much, because . . .
Rachael	Because the competent woman always has a better idea. She knows how to do it more quickly.
Diana	And a lot of times she does.
Rachael	Yeah!
Diana	So it's easier for everyone, but it's just feeding her sin.
Rachael	Yes, and she doesn't need me. Or maybe it's that she doesn't want me? There's a difference between need and want. Which one is more powerful to your soul as a woman—that you need people or that you want them? In my mind, wanting someone seems wonderful, and so invitational. I'd like to say to people, "I want you to come into my life. I want you to be in my life."
Sonya	It's easier for a competent woman to need somebody than to want somebody, and I think as a woman softens and becomes more inviting, she will want more.
Diana	Sometimes it's hard for me to distinguish between what I need and what I want.
Sonya	Maybe being competent says, "You better come through for me. Get it done." It's a need with a demand. Whereas the invitational part, which you offered that

recent night to your friends, was more of an invitation for them to come into your life and to be with you in it. And that was something you wanted.

Diana It was.

Rachael But you had to crack the door. You had to open the door to invite them in, and you did that very well. You offered your friends an invitation to enjoy not just what you can do, but who you are.

Sonya Yes, and as we're getting close to the end, that's the question that's running through my head; how do we as women move toward offering more than competency? I know what I want to be, but how do I move toward becoming more invitational, a lovely old woman someday, and invite people into my heart?

Rachael I think you still want to be a competent woman, but you have to give the softer side. You still should be competent—that's how you're made, that's who you are, that's how you think.

Sonya It just serves a different purpose. I want my competency to move in a direction that would love people, not impress people.

Rachael That's right, the competency remains, it's just used for something different than finding life and love apart from Christ. The word *competency* can be a good word.

Sonya Yes. I mean, I can't go make myself incompetent.

Rachael That's right, and you better not!

Diana Your family and friends and clients wouldn't want you to.

Sonya	But I want it to serve a different purpose. I don't want it to serve the purpose of impressing people, getting them to see how many things I can get in one counseling session. I want people to think, *She really loves me.* I want my competency to serve the purpose of the gospel. To pour myself out for the sake of others and to humbly receive the gift of people's lives.
Diana	Yes, I don't want to use competency to promote my abilities and protect myself. I want to give with abandon and receive with humility so that others can taste and see Christ in me.
Sonya	Being competent with the purpose of impressing or hiding is sin.
Rachael	Oh, yeah.
Diana	It's completely self-centered.
Sonya	I think when that stops me, I can go to repentance. I can drink deeply of God's grace. And I think my competence, which could do great harm, becomes a source of great good.
Diana	It's scary, you know, to let competence be for God's purposes, not to keep me feeling good. That's a big risk for me. It's worked so well for so long. But you're helping me see a new and better hope.

REFLECTING ON MY EXPERIENCE: DIANA

The idea that my competence could be offered with an invitation to something more was a new and wonderful thought to me. I recognized that as evidence of the power of Christ and the Spirit's presence in our conversation. When Sonya asked how this topic of competence relates to the gospel, I got excited! She reminded me of the great joy I found in the good news of the new life offered to me in Christ, and the "gift of God" that salvation was and is (Ephesians 2:8).

I know the Spirit is at work in me when I have conversations like these and I see things in new ways—both my sin and my hope in Christ. The gospel is particularly offensive, and equally freeing, to those of us who cling so tightly to our own competence. I want to control; Christ says rest in him. I want to impress; Christ's example in his death and resurrection is utter humility and perfect glory. I want relationship on my terms; Christ provides the only way to relationship with the Father.

Rachael, Sonya and I talked about a number of ways competence can be a barrier in relationships, and we also realized it wasn't the competence that was a problem but the way competence was used—to hide, to impress, to control. When I told them about my experience with confessing to some friends and inviting them to see me, they celebrated with me, and I began to hope for more of that kind of movement in other relationships.

I know it is ridiculously arrogant, but sometimes I try to bring my competence even to my relationship with God. I struggle with feeling like I am the lone exception on the planet to God's ability to offer unlimited mercy and grace through the person and power of Jesus Christ. In those times, I figure there's something that I can and must do to be worthy of his love. Talking with Sonya and Rachael helped me repent of that and see again that God is honored when I come to him, not in my competence but in humility and brokenness. He likes it when I ask for help. It gives him great pleasure and glory when I recognize and worship him as the One who gives and sustains life, and when I invite others into his life and love.

Learning to Listen In

For Reflection or Small Group Discussion

Ingredient 1. Identify an Intentional Purpose

Diana, Rachael and Sonya had different opinions about the implications of the word *competent*. Their purpose was to determine what that word means in various contexts, and how competence is offered makes the difference in whether it invites into or hinders the kingdom of God.

- What is an area where others would describe you as competent?

- When do you find your competence inviting people in? When does it push people away?

- When you are competent, does it invite people in or push people away?

- What would people learn about Christ and his love from the way you live out your competencies?

Ingredient 2. Tune In to Present Experience

Diana shared a story about a time when other friends had seen her sin and loved her. When Sonya made the connection between this time with her friends, competency and the gospel, Diana began to have a new picture of God's grace and love, the work of Christ and the power of the Spirit—apart from anything she could do on her own—and she began to experience renewed hope and joy.

- Read the book of Ephesians and consider how to invite the gospel into your next conversation.
- Ask Sonya's question: What connection does _____ (whatever topic you are discussing) have to the gospel?

Ingredient 3. Be Curious and Offer Feedback
In this conversation Diana's friends showed their curiosity not simply by asking questions (though there was some of that) but also by staying with the topic and offering Diana their own observations of how they saw new possibilities for using competency in inviting, unselfish ways.

- How might sharing your own experience offer helpful feedback in a conversation with a friend?
- When do you use it as a way to talk about yourself or to get the focus on you?

Ingredient 4. Explore Shaping Events
Sonya and Rachael shared examples of shaping events when they had tried to use competency for selfish reasons. They both used their competency to impress, and in conversation with friends Diana used her competency to hide.

- What events come to mind when you think about experiences with competency (or lack of competency)?
- What did you hope being competent would provide for you?
- Would the others in that event say your competence was inviting or off-putting? Why?

Ingredient 5. Create a Vision

Repentance is a word that scares some people, but it is the necessary beginning of any kingdom vision. When Sonya saw that using competence to impress or hide is sin, she spoke of repentance as the way toward "drinking his grace" and living different, being competent for the sake of others and more clearly reflecting Christ's invitation of love.

- What do you need to repent of?
- What keeps you from repentance?
- What leads you to repentance?
- In the forgiveness of Christ and through the work of the Spirit, what could be different about how you relate to others?

7

Reflecting on the Process

As I (Rachael) write this closing chapter, I have Mozart masterpieces playing in the background. Several memories are coming to mind: playing viola in the York Youth Symphony and high school orchestra, and my father coming out of a performance by the Cleveland Symphony Orchestra. On that special night I remember him saying: "That was the best worship service I've ever been in." Music has always drawn something out of me, mostly tears, and I am not one to tear up easily. I guess that's why I like using musical metaphors.

Ruthie Petit, an early reader of this manuscript, said it reminded her of a musical memory corresponding to our underlying theme of three voices, one song. She had attended a performance at the Walt Disney Concert Hall in Los Angeles with her classical trombonist son, Matthew Lawrence. Mitsuku Uchida was guest performer, and a commentary described her as "a performer who brings a deep insight into the music she plays through her own search for truth and beauty." My friend also shared,

> That same night, a new piece was debuted by a composer whose name escapes me. To my ear, it was a cacophony of sound without structure, coherence or melody. The composer had retrofitted the instruments in such a way that though there were notes being played; they were coming out of the instruments in a way that was not according to their original design. French horns had reeds instead of mouthpieces; notes were played in such a way that was offensive even to my untrained ear. There was a feeling of chaos and "out-of-syncness."

As I have thought about her story it has occurred to me that it was a picture of our lives still in the image of God but not aware of the gospel and the love of the Trinity, and the use of our instruments (us) in bringing glory to him, being set aright and moving into the lives of others according to his plan.

I believe that God has this experience constantly. He knows the beauty of the piece and sees the practicing and what every movement by each instrument, together and out of tune, is doing, and he fits it all into his plan. He rejoices at every off-pitch note, squeak and squawk, because he knows how these fit and will sound when not only redeemed but restored to our perfect design!

All these memories coincide with my perception of the several-year writing project Diana, Sonya and I have been composing. Like Uchida, we are searching for the truth and beauty in each of us. Writing with two others is definitely like being a part of an orchestra. Each member of the orchestra plays her instrument and follows her part—all different, yet, when practiced and tuned to the note given by the Concertmaster, lovely. God truly is the One to whom each of our voices (instruments) must be tuned. We worked to play our parts in concert with one another. Tuning was done in community, and personal tuning was done with much practice and understanding of the piece to be played. When three voices came together, we began to attune our hearts to the One with perfect love, and we began to work through the compositions of our relationships, putting together a piece that would more closely resemble the songs of the Trinity and their way of relating to each other.

When I think of the Trinity I am awed by their perichoretic (*peri* meaning "around" and *choretic* closely related to "choreograph") dancing around each other in a perfect way of relating. I have always found relationships of three the hardest to navigate, yet here I was writing with two others. We wrote this chapter to take you behind the scenes to see that we all need to be in the practice room. ("I am again in the pains of childbirth until Christ is formed in you" [Galatians 4:19].) At times it was difficult to get in tune with each other. We edited out some tension in conversations after one of our readers mentioned that although the tension was honest, it took her off in the direction of thinking about the intention behind that comment rather than the subject at hand. The reality is that we had tensions, some unspoken, some spoken; and another reality is we believe in each other, enough to stay in relationship with each other by having a vision for the good beneath the junk we could see in each other. This is the point at which we can relationally sin against the other (putting our interest above another), which goes contrary to the nature of God. We better reveal his nature by loving well as we see what God is redeeming in others and how they reflect his glory. With all that in mind we decided to end this chapter by modeling how to create a vision for each other.

Ingredient 5 is to create a vision. Before I create a vision statement for each of my two friends, I pray, listen to the Spirit on behalf of each of them and discern whether what I'm thinking may dredge up past hurts, is said to make me look good or for them to change to meet my expectations, or whether I am merely speaking Christianese, where I say something spiritually nice but with no depth. I trust you "listen in" and think about your conversations in light of other-centered relating, and the practice it takes to imitate the Trinity.

VISION LETTERS

Dear Sonya,

As I pray for you, lifting you up into the center of the Trinity, Isaiah 35:7 comes to mind: "The burning sand will become a pool, the thirsty ground bubbling springs." Why does that verse come to mind? During the past twenty years that I have been with you I have heard your parched soul wanting God to fill you with the water of his "loveliness" (your word).

We've known each other twenty years, but this writing project has provided the special blessing of getting to *know* you in a richer way. I found out that your past has creased your mind and heart with the word *different*, not a life word (Proverbs 18:21), and that you wore a football uniform to hide and protect your thirsty soul and mask that deep, lovely part of who you were made to be, a fully unique, inviting female. You've replaced the uniform with using your good mind to keep people at a distance by overprocessing relationships with family, friends, clients and others, and you just can't find the switch to turn off your brain. Sonya, you have a parched soul and that does not allow you to be comfortable in the truth that there is a beauty in that soul put there years ago by your heavenly Father.

My vision for you is that you'll rest in *him* and reflect that restful, Spirit-drenched, good soul, and that it will gush springs of living water overflowing with loveliness, rest, encouragement and beauty to all who come into your radiant presence. Your redeemed word is *unique*—that's what you are, unique: unique in that you have a hunger to learn and to give, to learn all that you can about living the life of Jesus and to give yourself as an invitation to others to live that life with you.

Publilius Syrus once said that many receive advice, only the wise profit by it. This is not advice, just a vision of who you already are, a unique woman who is at rest.

I love you, my lovely, restful friend. It's not over; the best is yet to come. The desert will become a pool, and the thirsty ground a bubbling brook. You will enter people rather than process conversations.

From an older friend on the journey who loves you and sees your loveliness from the inside out,
Rachael

Dear Diana,

Irenaeus once said that the glory of God is a human being fully alive. As I sat quietly to reflect on you in the midst of the Trinity, those words from Irenaeus popped into my mind. Seventeen years ago, when we first met on the Moscow ministry trip, you stood out as a sharp, competent woman (if I remember correctly, you were on that trip to teach in one of the Russian schools?) and in the years of this writing project God's gift to you of competency has been evident: you think, write and edit very well. What I didn't know was that *competent* was a word long used by others and by you to define who you are, but during this project you realized that it does not define your femininity.

You have always been a "take charge kind of gal," and the good in that statement is that you do a wonderful job of taking charge of projects. You are unusually perceptive in your assessments of things. Hmm, very competent.

The redeemed word that came out of our time together is *invitational*, and getting pictures of your new hairdo, seeing you primp before going home after one of our writing trips, and wanting opinions on what looks good on you is all so inviting even to me, a friend. It gives me hope that I don't have to compete with your competency.

My vision for you is that you'll be released: released to cry deep tears, released to show emotional tenderness and released to have a few good belly laughs. My dear Diana, release what is in you that draws others to enjoy you. God has made you a beautiful, kind, tender woman who also happens to be quite capable. Let everyone see that invitational wife, mom, coworker and friend. It will help you to rest and to overcome your need to take charge, and to release you to give to God and others what is most beautiful—*you*.

With love from one who believes in you,
Rachael

Sonya and Diana also wrote vision letters not included here.

NEXT STEPS

You now have a feel for conversations that matter in the kingdom. You will never be content with surface conversations again! The questions after the chapters have been "practice" for having similar conversations with your own group of like-minded women. If you sense it is time to start your own journey of life-changing conversations, here is a map to get started.

1. Pray about whom to invite (no more than three or four).

2. Set a time and place to meet.

3. Have each woman write a story that has shaped her view of herself and life in general.

4. One person reads her story aloud (only one story per meeting).

5. Discuss that story as you follow the five ingredients mentioned in the introduction.

   - Be in touch with what you are feeling as your friend speaks about her life.

   - Be curious about what might lie beneath the surface of her words.

   - Be willing to share honestly and kindly what you observe.

   - Invite her to tell stories that seem to have shaped who she has become and how she lives out her femininity in the world, especially in her relationships.

   - Share your vision for her. Tell your hope for her and give her a picture of what she could be as she falls more in love with the Savior.

6. Decide together what might be the theme in the speaker's story (such as Sonya's "differentness" or Diana's "competence" and Rachael's "voicelessness"). Talk about how the past might be influencing present-day relating.

7. End with a commitment to pray about your conversations during the next meeting.

8. At your second meeting, center your conversation around the theme of the first speaker's story and its impact in each of your lives. (Perhaps write down thoughts that come to you as the week progresses so you can share how your friend has affected your own life.)

9. At the third meeting another person reads her story aloud, and the group follows the same steps.

10. After all stories have been shared, plan to have a session of celebration (perhaps a dinner out or a tea party) to rejoice in what God has done to deepen your love for him and for each other.

Afterword

Man to Man

By Larry Crabb

If somehow this book by women for women has made its way into your hands, and if you've turned to this appendix and are deciding whether to read it, let me quickly say two things. One, it's brief, so it won't require much of your time. And, two, what I have to say might encourage you to relate better to the women in your life.

If your wife gave you this book, she has given you the opportunity to understand what she longs to receive from others, what she can receive from you, and what she can better receive from other women. My wife, Rachael, one of the three authors of this book, meets regularly with at least three different groups of women. I've come to realize that these meetings are doing for her what I cannot do, what other women are better equipped to do. I therefore encourage and support her participation. Our marriage has been strengthened because of what she both gives and receives in her small groups with other women.

I hope this book finds its way into the hands of pastors. If you are a pastor reading these words, let me urge you to keep reading. If the women in your church begin meeting together in ways this book both models and suggests, your church community will be stronger. Relationships will deepen and families will grow healthier.

Pastors, advocate for soul-to-soul community among women. Too often, women meeting in small groups feel marginalized, sensing that church leadership thinks *more* important things are happening. Encourage women to realize that of course *other* important things are taking place, but that you believe in the important value of women meeting to discuss the relationship between their faith in Christ and the unique challenges and opportunities of their femininity as God-designed females.

I hope, too, that counselors will read "listen in." I've been a psychologist for more than forty years, and, as is typical, more than half of the folks I've counseled over those years have been women. The stories unfolded in the conversations recorded in this book will help male counselors particularly to hear the deep pain in women's souls and to more fully appreciate the power of relationships to awaken the joy beneath the pain that only the gospel of Christ provides.

When our wives completed this book, we three husbands met for a day to discuss the impact we could see in our wives. Dave, Sonya's husband, John, married to Diana, and I, coming up on fifty years of marriage to Rachael, agreed that our wives had been visibly and very positively impacted through their many months of rich conversations. They were becoming more alive as women, and we realized we were given the opportunity to step up as men. Speaking for myself, living with Rachael as she related with Diana and Sonya in the process of writing this book, I've seen more of her beautiful substance emerge as a generous, gifted, inviting and confident woman. Not only has my love for her deepened, but my respect has grown as well. The conversations to which others can now listen in have continued to mature my wife into an increasingly godly woman.

Men—whether husband, father, pastor, counselor or friend— let me urge you to read this book. You'll better understand the women in your life. And you'll more fully appreciate how you can encourage the Spirit's work in their lives as they meet together as women to speak life into each other.

Acknowledgments

Thank you from Rachael . . .

Larry: My beloved. Guardian of my heart, champion of my world, my partner in ministry and life. My best friend for five decades, who has been so supportive of this project even while he works on his own.

Kep and Kimmie, Ken and Lesley: My sons and daughters-in-law, whose commitment to God and unyielding dedication to each other and their children brings joy and pride to my heart.

My precious grands: Josie, Jake, Kaitlyn, Keira and Kensington: you are in my heart with lots of love.

My siblings: Carolyn (deceased), Ann, Lowell and Philip (deceased), you are at the beginning of my story and a huge part of my continually developing story. I love you!

My covenant sisters: You helped me get an authentic voice by listening: Elisa, Ellen, Donna, Judie, Linda, Ruth and Verna. Girlfriends, too many to name, in the birthday groups, book clubs and Bible studies, all part of my story.

The Intentional Spiritual Formation Group: We struggle together in community, Bob, Claudia, Tom and Jenny, and Larry, to make sense of the bit part in *his*tory that we are to play. "I thank my God every time I remember you!" (Philippians 1:3).

Thank you from Sonya . . .

Always a part of who I am becoming: My Mom, Nancy, and my Dad, Larry, the Bradys, the Marshalls, the Hensleys, the Fitzsimmons, Whitney, the Lawrences, the Shores, the Reeders, the Crabbs, CBC friends, Amy (my adopted daughter), Erin, Jennie, Jill, my LCC family and care group, and to those who have trusted me to listen in to their stories.

Jason: My little brother, thanks for enduring mac-n-cheese and a bossy sister. I love you Christine, Garrett and Olivia.

Anne: You will forever be my "heart sister."

The Allens: You were "home" to me, and it was there I learned manila folders weren't vanilla folders.

Helene, Jenny, Bev, Diana and Sharon: For many years you have modeled courageous beauty in how you live and you have helped that beauty to awaken in me.

Nancy: You are one of the truest pictures of real beauty I know, and the way you and Bill love me frees me to go and love better.

Joye: Your loyalty to me is unwavering, and your grace to me is my rare gift.

Joanie: Few people give like you do, and I could ask for no better friend. You are a safe place for me to be a mess, and you still love me.

Chase: You are the most warrior-like young man I know. Don't let winning battles mean more to you than your affection for Christ. Son, your courage is great and I love you.

Abigail: I love no other lady like I love you. You have one of the most beautiful hearts I have ever known. My dear daughter, may you let your beauty speak of his love and grace.

Ethan: You are my best surprise ever. Never have I seen a young man be as brave in his willingness to show kindness as I have you. May your brave heart stand strong for years to come for the sake of the gospel. Son, I love you.

David: Even after twenty-five years of marriage you are still my biggest fan. In all my unpredictable moods you meet me with steadiness and grace. You encourage my beauty to grow even at great cost to yourself. I love you.

Thank you from Diana . . .

My Trinity Fellowship Church family: I wish I could list every name and tell all the stories of God at work. We worship, suffer and celebrate as a body, and we share real life together for the glory of Christ. I'm so thankful for you.

Helene, Sharon, Bev, Jenny and Sonya: You help me to be a softer woman. Looking forward to many more conversations that matter.

HMC—John C., Keith and Beth, John and Dana: The way you make yourselves known moves me toward the Father's love. Emma, Isaac, Luke, Trey, Elissa, Ethan and Emily—you're the best. And the food's pretty good too.

Mom and Ken, Daria and Dane: You continue to be God's great gifts of grace to me.

Emily: I love being your mom. When you speak out of the center of your heart, your beauty is stunning. You show me what it's like to be full of life. Watching you grow brings your dad and me such delight.

John: I would rather be with you than anyone else in this world. You see me with remarkable clarity and deep perception, and when you tell me what you see, you lead me into the love of Christ. And nobody makes me laugh like you. I love you with all my heart.

Thank you from Rachael, Sonya and Diana . . .

Joanie: You hosted us for many getaways, just to work on this project. Your support was and is so encouraging.

Tom and Susan: You so graciously provided us with another place to retreat.

Karen: You transcribed conversation recordings to get us print copies to work from.

Marcia: You prayed over this project and contributed support in ways that are only known to us.

Readers: You helped by taking time to read and comment as we completed chapters. You got us thinking critically and helped us with your insights.

Andi, from NewWay Ministries: You tirelessly gave of your knowledge and time to help us focus.

Holly Benyouski, Street Level Agency, Warsaw, IN: You heard about this project and asked if you could see it. You took it to Jeff Crosby, Jeff gave it to Cindy Bunch with IVP Crescendo, and the rest is history . . .

Cindy Bunch, a wonderful new friend, and the IVP team who encouraged, edited and brought the book to life.

Patti Smith, editor. It's been a many-year journey! Thank you for really taking it across the finish line.

Thank you to the one God—Father, Son and Spirit—for being worthy of our worship and service, and for extending your overflowing life to us. We pray that through this book we would serve you well.

Reflections from Readers

We asked some women to "listen in" as we wrote the manuscript for this project. Their reactions moved, inspired and motivated us to continue on with the call to model for others the symphony of conversation when it is lead by the Holy Spirit.

You often hear that we as women struggle, but there is something so hopeful in hearing it shared personally, especially by three spiritual women who are walking ahead of me in life. I felt inspired to keep going, to look to Jesus for continued change like all three of you women so obviously do. Your conversations were different and struck me as solid, of substance and regarding first things. —*Sarah*

Your conversations show pursuit, messiness, awkwardness and a vision for your friend to become more like Christ. I loved that. —*Judy*

I felt so many things while reading—I could relate so well to each story. You all were able to find the common threads of female experience and bring it out in a casual conversation about significant stories from your childhoods. I felt so stirred/encouraged by what I read, that I actually sat down for several hours and typed out some of my own stories. I think I just wanted to reconnect with me as a little girl and see what happened. It was very freeing, and I don't think I'm done. —*Jenny*

The stories you've each contributed speak to issues many women face. You touched on power and control in relationships, being open about vulnerabilities, having a voice, and feeling like you're just too much, among other things. I can imagine your readers being curious about that for themselves and for their friends as well. They may be listening in to your conversations, but I can picture them starting conversations of their own. —*Rachel*

I loved how you were each invited to live out of the beautiful, redeemed parts of the story. Each of you has an experience that is painful and taught you how to try to make life work. What is amazing is how each "weakness" is reflected as a beautiful strength, once redeemed. I am so excited to see how God will use this to encourage women to bravely look into their own hearts and gently look into the hearts of other women to draw out the loveliest parts of themselves—to learn to let God redeem our stories and move us out of the sinful places we've been operating from. —*Jennie*

IVP *Crescendo*
COURAGE. CONFIDENCE. CALLING.

Some voices challenge us. Others support or encourage us. Voices can move us to change our minds, draw close to God, discover a new spiritual gift. The voices of others are shaping who we are.

The voices behind IVP Crescendo join together to draw us into God's story. We'll discover God's work around the globe even as we learn to love the people around the corner. We'll have opportunity to heal our places of pain. We'll discover new ways to love our families. We'll hear God's voice speaking into our lives as we discover new places of influence.

IVP Crescendo invites you to join in the rising chorus

- *to listen to the voices of others*
- *to hear the voice of God*
- *and to grow your own voice in*

COURAGE. CONFIDENCE. CALLING.

ivpress.com/crescendo
ivpress.com/crescendo-social